PSYCHOANALYTIC PSYCHOTHERAPY
IN THE
INDEPENDENT TRADITION

Also edited by Stanley Ruszczynski & Sue Johnson
and published by Karnac Books:

PSYCHOANALYTIC PSYCHOTHERAPY IN THE KLEINIAN TRADITION

PSYCHOANALYTIC PSYCHOTHERAPY

IN THE

INDEPENDENT TRADITION

edited by

Sue Johnson & Stanley Ruszczynski

London

KARNAC BOOKS

The work illustrated on the front cover is reproduced by kind permission of the Henry Moore Foundation.

Figures 9 and 10 (reprinted on p. 97) from *Through Peadiatrics to Psychoanalysis* by D. W. Winnicott. London: Hogarth Press, and copyright © 1958 by Basic Books, a member of Perseus Books, L.L.C. Reprinted by permission of Random House UK Ltd. and of Basic Books.

First published in 1999 by
H. Karnac (Books) Ltd.
58 Gloucester Road
London SW7 4QY

British Library Cataloguing in Publication Data

A C.I.P. record for this book is available from the British Library.

ISBN 1-85575-176-3

Edited, designed, and produced by Communication Crafts

Printed in Great Britain by Polestar Wheatons Ltd, Exeter

10 9 8 7 6 5 4 3 2 1

To Mike,
and Stella, Jamie, and Helen

ACKNOWLEDGEMENTS

We would like to sincerely thank all the authors for their chapters, often written in holiday time, or in precious free time, or between patients, teaching commitments, and other professional activities, whilst also trying to live life! We would also like to thank them for bearing with us both in our pressurizing them and then in our long silences as we tried to get on with the editing. We hope that they will be as pleased as we are with the end result.

We are very grateful to Cesare Sacerdoti and Graham Sleight and their team at Karnac Books for patiently waiting for this book and its sister volume, *Psychoanalytic Psychotherapy in the Kleinian Tradition*, published at the same time. Cesare Sacerdoti's sensitive but realistic understanding and forbearance of the shortcomings of psychotherapists trying to write, edit, and publish and his commitment to this project encouraged and sustained us. We are also indebted to Klara and Eric King for their skilful part in the production of these books.

We would like to thank those friends and colleagues who encouraged us and shared our excitement, and especially Faith Miles, who was particularly helpful. We would like to acknowledge the British Association of Psychotherapists, which trained us and which makes up an important part of our professional lives. We are especially grateful to our personal psychoanalysts and to those who supervised our clinical work during our training.

On behalf of the contributors to this volume, we thank all of our patients, without whom this book could not have been written. We have made every effort to disguise clinical material so as to ensure anonymity and to use only that that is absolutely necessary for purposes of illustration. Through writing this book, the authors want to describe to colleagues their ways of thinking about their clinical experiences. The purpose of this is to go on learning through developing theoretical understanding of, and therefore clinical work with, those people who come to our consulting-rooms.

CONTENTS

CONTRIBUTORS

RUTH BERKOWITZ is a Full Member of the British Association of Psychotherapists and has a full-time private practice of psychoanalytic psychotherapy. She was formerly in clinical research at the Maudsley and Friern Hospitals and trained as a family therapist at the Tavistock Clinic. She is involved in training and teaching at the British Association of Psychotherapists. She has published papers on schizophrenia, family therapy, and psychoanalytic psychotherapy.

JUDY COOPER is a Full Member of the British Association of Psychotherapists and is in private practice as a psychoanalytic psychotherapist and supervisor. She is the author of *Speak of Me as I Am: The Life and Work of Masud Khan* (London: Karnac Books, 1993); co-editor (with Nilda Maxwell) of *Narcissistic Wounds: Clinical Perspectives* (London: Whurr Publishers, 1995), and co-editor (with Helen Alfille) of *Assessment in Psychotherapy* (London: Karnac Books, 1998), as well as the author of various book chapters and journal papers. She also lectures and teaches.

SUE JOHNSON is a Full Member of the British Association of Psychotherapists and has a full-time private practice of psychoanalytic psychotherapy and supervision. She had previously been employed part-time as a psychotherapist at the Brandon Centre for Counselling and Psychotherapy for Young People where she worked with adolescents and their families. She teaches on a number of courses for the British Association of Psychotherapists.

JOSCELYN RICHARDS is a Chartered Clinical Psychologist and a Full Member of the British Association of Psychotherapists and the British Psychological Society. She has served on the Council of the BAP and was recently Chair of their Psychoanalytic Psychotherapy Training Committee. She is on the Council of the Association for Psychoanalytic Psychotherapy in the NHS and has been Chairman of the British Confederation of Psychotherapists since its inauguration in 1993. She has a small private practice, but much of her work is in the public sector, where she is Lead Clinician in Psychotherapy and Consultant Clinical Psychologist at the Willesden Centre for Psychological Treatment. She undertakes clinical teaching at the Willesden Centre and for the BAP. She has presented and written papers on clinical work and the organization of psychotherapy services.

VIQUI ROSENBERG is a Full Member of the British Association of Psychotherapists and is in full-time private practice. She has been a part-time tutor of psychodynamic counselling at Birkbeck College and an external examiner and tutor on various psychotherapy and counselling trainings. She currently teaches in the professional course of the British Association of Psychotherapists.

STANLEY RUSZCZYNSKI is a Full Member of the British Association of Psychotherapists and has a part-time private practice of psychoanalytic psychotherapy. He is a Principal Adult Psychotherapist at the Portman Clinic (Tavistock and Portman NHS Trust), London. He is a founder Member of the Society of Psychoanalytic Marital Psychotherapists and for a number of years was a senior member of staff in the Tavistock Marital Studies Institute (Tavistock Centre), London, serving as Deputy Director and both Clinical and Training Co-ordinator. He is the editor of *Psychotherapy with*

Couples (Karnac Books, 1993), co-editor (with James Fisher) of *Intrusiveness and Intimacy in the Couple* (Karnac Books, 1995), as well as the author of a number of book chapters and journal papers. He undertakes clinical teaching for the British Association of Psychotherapists.

ANNE TYNDALE is a Full Member and Training Therapist and Supervisor for the British Association of Psychotherapists. She works in private practice in Brighton.

ANNA WITHAM is a Full Member of the British Association of Psychotherapists and has a full-time private practice of psychoanalytic psychotherapy and supervision. Prior to this she had been a Senior Lecturer in Psychology at the then North East London Polytechnic, now the University of East London. She is at present the Registrar of the British Confederation of Psychotherapists.

PSYCHOANALYTIC PSYCHOTHERAPY
IN THE
INDEPENDENT TRADITION

Introduction

Sue Johnson & Stanley Ruszczynski

T he authors of the chapters in this book identify themselves as psychoanalytic psychotherapists whose work is influenced by the Independent Tradition of the British School of Psychoanalysis. This tradition has been written about extensively by both Gregorio Kohon and Eric Rayner (Kohon, 1986a; Rayner, 1991).

Certain characteristics of the Independent Tradition will be recognizable in this volume. Firstly, there exists within that Tradition a basic recognition and acceptance of the importance of early infant development and of the relationship between the infant and the mother. It then follows that in current Independent-influenced psychoanalytic psychotherapy, the analysis of the individual patient's psychopathology will be balanced by the analysis of the relationship between the patient and therapist, with the emphasis on examining and attempting to understand what occurs between the two in the "transitional area" of the psychotherapeutic treatment.

In a number of his writings, Donald Winnicott refers to the time at a Scientific Meeting of the British Psycho-Analytical Soci-

1

ety (circa 1940) when he excitedly made the statement, "There is no such thing as a baby (infant)" (Winnicott, 1947, p. 137; 1952a, p. 99; 1960d, p. 39). He says that he was alarmed by his statement and went on to try to justify himself "by pointing out that if you show me a baby you certainly show me also someone caring for the baby, or at least a pram with someone's eyes and ears glued to it. One sees a 'nursing couple'" (Winnicott, 1952a, p. 99). In the context of the therapeutic treatment, Winnicott's statement can be extended to: "There is no such thing as a patient" or, alternatively, from the opposite position, "There is no such thing as a therapist".

The reader of this volume will come across other familiar concepts developed by writers within the Tradition in their attempts to understand early infant development—Michael Balint's "basic fault", W. Ronald D. Fairbairn's "internal saboteur", Winnicott's "true and false self", "continuity of being", "holding" and "holding environment", "good-enough mother", and "transitional space", to name but a few.

A second hallmark of the Independent Tradition is the refusal to adhere to any inflexible system of theory, but to draw instead on a number of existing psychoanalytic concepts and ways of thinking and to continue to develop and elaborate on them. It is not surprising, therefore, to find that the Independent Tradition is replete with paradox. The authors who write here are happy to draw on existing concepts from the broad range of psychoanalytic theory. For confirmation of this, one has only to look at the list of references at the end of the book, which includes not only the names of numerous Independent writers, but also many references to Sigmund Freud, Sándor Ferenczi, and Heinrich Racker, as well as Kleinian writers such as Wilfred Bion, Ronald Britton, Robert Hinshelwood, Betty Joseph, Herbert Rosenfeld, Hanna Segal, John Steiner, and Melanie Klein herself.

It is for this very reason that the authors of these chapters, in keeping with the Tradition, sometimes pose unsettling questions about existing psychoanalytic tenets and at other times attempt to extend established psychoanalytic theory. Some of the questions raised in this volume are:

• May the false self of the patient be paralleled by the analytic neutrality of the therapist, and if so, what are the implications of this?

• What existing theory sufficiently explains a patient who appears to have two separate personalities, or is a new theory needed?

• How far is transference interpretation essential to psychic change?

• When does a therapist become a "traumatogenic object" and reproduce trauma in the treatment?

The first four chapters in the book are concerned with early development and environmental failure—two areas that are given prominent attention by the Independent School.

In the opening two chapters, Sue Johnson and Joscelyn Richards are concerned with psychic structures that either are present or develop in earliest infancy. In Chapter 1, "Who and Whose I Am: The Emergence of the True Self", Sue Johnson offers a clinical account of an intensive psychoanalytic psychotherapy treatment with a woman whom she had had in treatment for just under ten years. She describes the regression in the treatment that led to the eventual emergence of the patient's true self. She relies heavily on Winnicott's well-known true self/false self (Winnicott, 1960b) conceptualization to form the basis of her theoretical stance, and she questions the viability of maintaining an "analytically neutral" stance when working with patients who display a marked false self.

Chapter 2, "The Concept of Internal Cohabitation", by Joscelyn Richards, is also essentially about a split in the personality. In contrast to Sue Johnson, who uses a recognized concept from the Independent Tradition in her theoretical description, Joscelyn Richards finds traditional Kleinian and Independent concepts, including Winnicott's true-self/false-self concept, to be inadequate when attempting to account for the phenomena she encountered in the mental life of patients with whom she was working. Instead, she posits the concept of "internal cohabitation" (Sinason, 1993), which was developed by Michael Sinason, Richards, and colleagues. She presents detailed clinical material from work with a patient to illustrate how she uses the concept.

In Chapter 3, Anne Tyndale poses the controversial question, "How Far Is Transference Interpretation Essential to Psychic Change?" She draws extensively on writings from the Independent Tradition, and she questions one of the basic tenets of psychoanalytic theory, that of the importance of transference interpretation. Tyndale refers to Joseph (1985), who notes that transference phenomena apply to the whole therapeutic setting and not only the therapist himself, and she develops her point further by discussing the interpretation of transference phenonema that relate to people other than the therapist. She stresses the importance of respecting the limitations imposed upon the work by the patient and the need for the therapist to forego therapeutic ambition. She argues that significant but limited psychic change came about in one of her patients, despite her patient's refusal to engage in exploration of the negative transference.

In Chapter 4, "The Absent Mother: Splitting as a Narcissistic Attempt to Find a Solution", Judy Cooper also addresses the theme of the limitation of psychotherapeutic work. Rather than concentrating on the interpretative technique, however, she writes about the partial solutions she had to accept when working with a severely narcissistic patient whom she had had in a long-term intensive treatment. She presents extensive clinical material from the treatment to illustrate how the absence of an emotionally present mother contributes to splitting, which is one facet of the narcissistic solution. Cooper, like Richards, draws on both Kleinian and Independent conceptualization as well as the writings of Freud and Strachey in her extended clinical account.

In writing about the limitations of psychotherapeutic work, Tyndale and Cooper follow Freud himself. In Lecture 34 of the *New Introductory Lectures on Psycho-Analysis* he wrote:

> The therapeutic effectiveness of psychoanalysis remains cramped by a number of weighty and scarcely assailable factors. . . . In the case of adults the difficulties arise in the first instance from two factors: the amount of psychical rigidity present and the form of the illness with all that that covers in the way of deeper determinants. [Freud, 1933a, p. 154]

The next two chapters are linked in two ways. First, both authors write in detail about a specific aspect of the therapeutic process. Second, they both reflect on analytic technique and the potential for acting out in the countertransference when working in the areas they discuss.

In Chapter 5, "The Move from Object-Relating to Object-Usage: A Clinical Example", Sue Johnson begins by tracing the development of Winnicott's ideas on aggression and destruction over a period of thirty years, which culminated in his classic paper, "The Use of an Object and Relating Through the Use of Identifications" (Winnicott, 1971a). She then presents material from a long-term treatment to illustrate her understanding of how this move from object relating towards object-usage came about initially in the transference. She concludes by emphasizing the importance of assessing the patient's stage of ego-integration and discusses the technical difficulties when working with a patient who is functioning at the level Winnicott defines as "pre-integration" (Winnicott, 1950–1955).

In Chapter 6, "The Potential for Trauma in the Transference and Countertransference", Ruth Berkowitz extends the views Michael Balint put forward in his paper, "Trauma and Object Relations" (Balint, 1969). This is a little-quoted paper in which Balint develops his understanding of "the finer dynamics of traumatogenesis". After examining the thinking on trauma put forward by various authors, she discusses in detail the three phases outlined in Balint's paper and the potential for trauma in the psychotherapeutic setting. She then uses a number of clinical vignettes to illustrate her understanding of the potential for the therapist to become the "traumatogenic object" and the work in the countertransference she believes necessary in order to avoid this happening.

The last two chapters in the volume, those of Viqui Rosenberg and Anna Witham, address oedipal and post-oedipal development.

Viqui Rosenberg explores the erotic, eroticized, and sexualized transferences in Chapter 7, "Erotic Transference and Its Vicissitudes in the Countertransference". She points to the relative scarcity of writing on the erotic transference and uses her anxieties associated with writing the chapter to form the basis of her formulations on the subject. Her chapter encompasses the two areas of life that Freud designated as being crucial—love and work.

Through clinical material she very clearly illustrates the appearance of the erotic transference in the treatment and describes its effect on her and the way in which she worked with it. She concludes her chapter with a section on the sublimation of the erotic transference and questions the part this plays when the patient decides to become a psychotherapist.

In Chapter 8, "Dreaming and Day-Dreaming", Anna Witham follows the Independent Tradition in her interest in creativity. She explores the sources of dreams and day-dreams and examines their relationships to the creative process. Through clinical material, she illustrates the use her patient makes of the creativity in a dream. She then contrasts this with another patient whose day-dream is defensive and provides only a substitute gratification. Her chapter is concerned with the area that Winnicott (1971a) and many other Independents consider to be a third area that is of equal importance to the two areas of love and work suggested by Freud—that of creativity and play.

Freud himself recognized the value of play. In "Remembering, Repeating and Working-Through", when writing about the repetition compulsion, he referred to the transference as a playground in which the repetition compulsion could be given complete freedom to expand and thereby be understood and given meaning (Freud, 1914g, p. 154). Winnicott developed this idea more fully and distinguished between "play" and "playing" (Winnicott, 1971a, 1971b, 1989). In his introduction to *Through Paediatrics to Psycho-Analysis*, Masud Khan (1975) writes that Winnicott's basic hypothesis can be given in the following two quotations.

> Psychotherapy takes place in the overlap of two areas of playing, that of the patient and that of the therapist. Psychotherapy has to do with two people playing together. The corollary of this is that where playing is not possible then the work done by the therapist is directed towards bringing the patient from a state of not being able to play into a state of being able to play.

and:

> Whatever I say about children playing really applies to adults as well, only the matter is more difficult to describe when the patient's material appears mainly in terms of verbal communication. I suggest that we must expect to find playing just as

evident in the analyses of adults as it is in the case of our work with children. It manifests itself, for instance, in the choice of works,[1] in the inflections of the voice, and indeed in the sense of humour. [Winnicott, cited in Khan, 1975, p. xxviii]

From its origin with Freud, psychoanalytic theory has continued to be developed by practitioners who struggle to make sense of the difficulties they encounter in their work. This volume contains a wealth of clinical material presented sometimes in the form of extended clinical accounts and at other times as vignettes. In keeping with the spirit of the Independent Tradition, the sequence of chapters follows a developmental line. The reader will encounter a diversity of topics and a disparity of ideas, inspired by the creativity inherent in that tradition. The single most important theme, however, is the concentration on the interplay between therapist and patient, both actively present in the consulting-room, engaged in examining their relationship in the "playground" of the transference.

Note

1. This is a misquotation of Winnicott, who wrote "words" and not "works" (D. W. Winnicott, *Playing and Reality*, p. 40 [Tavistock Publications, 1971]). However, this misquotation reminds us that our choice of work might well, in part, be unconsciously motivated by a search for an arena for playing, in Winnicott's sense, for bridging the internal and the external worlds. This would, of course, be especially true in the case of the work of psychoanalytic psychotherapy, both for the patient and for the clinician. This typographical error has been corrected in the 1999 reprint of Winnicott's *Through Paediatrics to Psycho-Analysis* (Karnac Books).

CHAPTER ONE

Who and whose I am:
the emergence of the true self

Sue Johnson

The title of this chapter is derived from a question posed to me at the beginning of a session recently by a woman whom I have been seeing for intensive psychoanalytic psychotherapy for just under a decade. Without her being aware of it at the time, the search for her "true self" (Winnicott, 1960b) was what had originally prompted her to seek treatment. Her desire to find conditions in the outside world that will allow for its expression is at the core of our continuing work together.

In this account I shall try to show how my attempt to maintain a stance of analytic neutrality occasionally resulted in false-self behaviour on my part and how my momentary movements away from that position both paralleled and facilitated the emergence of the true self of my patient.

Before introducing the reader to Janet, it is perhaps worth first introducing myself.

At the time that Janet was referred to me, I was newly qualified as a psychoanalytic psychotherapist, and I had been practising for approximately a year. I was working in an agency with adolescents and their families, and I had a small private practice.

9

In my previous work settings I had been required to make practical arrangements for clients, thereby involving me in more "real" contact, but I was keen to work in a more analytical way.

One dictionary definition of the word "neutrality"—the stance meant to be taken by a psychoanalytic psychotherapist—is: "absence of decided views, feeling, or expression, indifference; impartiality, dispassionateness" (Brown, 1993, p. 1911). My understanding of the phrase "analytic neutrality" came from Freud's statement, "The doctor should be opaque to his patients and, like a mirror, should show them nothing but what is shown to him" (Freud, 1912e, p. 118). At that time I took this to mean that I was to withhold anything personal about myself from my patients.

Looking back, I think it is fair to say that I took into the consulting-room something of a false self—what I then believed to be an analytically neutral one, but one that was, in fact, a false one. For the most part, I attempted to leave myself outside the consulting-room. It was the way in which, I believed, I would then not intrude into the analytic space that I provided for my patients. My experience was, I imagine, akin to that of Symington, who writes about how his narcissism as a beginning psychotherapist contributed to something of a "self-annihilation" when he was practising (Symington, 1996).

At this juncture the reader can probably see that this search for the true self was the point at which my patient and I met—she, searching to find her true self, I looking to find a way of expressing mine as a practising psychotherapist.

JANET

I will now introduce the reader to Janet.

Janet was 57 when she was referred to me by a consultant psychiatrist/psychotherapist at a therapeutic community. She had been a patient there for over three years following a breakdown several years previously, and she had recently made contact with him when she again found herself in difficulties. He recommended that she have intensive psychotherapy (minimum three times a week), and she readily accepted his suggestion. He told me that she came from the provinces and that she had grown up in a closely knit, intact family. Both of her parents had been dead for some years, as had her elder brother. She had two elder sisters, both of whom lived near her childhood home. She and her husband were both retired. She had been a teacher, and he a businessman. They had two grown-up sons. The referrer said that Janet's memory was extraordinarily vivid and that when she spoke of any past happening, it was as though it had only just happened. The detail of each remembered event was as clear as a bell.

Janet arrived on time for her initial consultation with me. I opened the door, to be greeted by an attractive woman with beautiful silver-blonde hair. She was well dressed and immaculately groomed. Her hair and appearance were striking because her face was youthful but her hair denoted age. Her voice was that of a sweet little girl.

I remember little of the content of my initial consultation with Janet, but my memory of the atmosphere and of her sense of urgency is vivid. She spoke quickly and was worried that I would not take her into treatment but would, instead, send her away. She told me she had had three breakdowns—the first being after her mother had died 20 years previously. She described the events surrounding her mother's death, just as my colleague had told me she would; it was as though no time had passed and she continued to be in deep grief.

Janet recalled being in her bedroom upstairs weeping when she and her family returned home after the funeral. Her husband came upstairs and reminded her that she had two little boys downstairs who needed her. At that moment she got up, put on a mask, and just carried on with life for the sake of her family. Since the year following her mother's death, she had had various forms of psychiatric treatment for depression, including hospitalization, medication, ECT, and three years in a psychoanalytically oriented therapeutic community, where she had experienced various forms of treatment. One statement she said to me forcefully was that I would have to push her out when the time came—she would not be able to go.

My experience of Janet was that she was studying my face to find something; her look was a plaintive, searching one, which, at the time, I experienced as intrusive in that it seemed to allow no thought to take place, either in her or in me. In *Diary of a Baby*

Stern says, when referring to 4½-month-old Joey: "After all, it is mainly in the face that we feel we can read one another's feelings and intentions. And we start becoming experts at the very beginning of our lives" (Stern, 1990, p. 48).

In addition to scrutinizing me, Janet also talked non-stop. At the same time, she appeared to be wanting something from me that I felt unable to give while she was controlling me through her gaze and her speech. My experience was that she wanted to relate to me in a very real way, which left me feeling unable to occupy my therapeutic space, and I think because she was so anxious to please me, she compliantly agreed to use the couch. I believe it is true to say that it was my need for some distance—for some "neutral territory"—that dictated my need for her to use the couch (Winnicott, 1950).

Janet had been referred to me in June. As there were only six weeks before the summer break, I offered, as is my usual practice in such a circumstance, to see her once a week until the break and to begin then seeing her three times a week when we resumed in September. Janet readily accepted this, but after the second week of treatment she asked whether I could see her twice a week or even three times a week until the break. At the time I sensed a desperation in her, so I agreed to it. The reason she gave was that her eldest son was to marry in October. He wanted the reception to be at the family home, and Janet had agreed, but she was very anxious about her ability to cope. She did not want to begin intensive treatment just before the wedding.

My memory of those first six weeks of treatment is dim, other than to say that Janet continued to talk rapidly, anxiously filling up the space. She seemed unable to pause for thought. I listened and seldom interpreted. I had little idea why she had been referred to me but relied on my colleague's assessment that intensive psychotherapy was the treatment of choice.

I have a distinct memory of being puzzled by one particular phrase Janet used. She talked in detail about individuals with whom she had grown up and, in describing people to me, she would occasionally say that the person was a "love-child". Each time she used the expression, she would anxiously sit up, turn around, and look directly at me, then resume her position lying down. I remember feeling perplexed as well as somewhat irritated by this. Clearly she was looking for something, but I had no idea what it was. I believe she probably sensed my irritation and then resumed her position to please me. Her sitting up appeared to have a defensive quality to it—it was as though she no longer wanted to think but wanted instead to relate. I, in my "neutral mode", tried to appear as unresponsive as possible in turn.

Janet returned from the summer break looking strained and tense. She sat on the couch and looked me straight in the eye. She said, "I have had a shock, and I knew I just had to hold on until you got back." I was briefly left in suspense while she lay down and began recounting the events of the break.

She had great difficulty in telling me what had happened. Her account was as follows. She and her husband had gone down to the village where she had grown up to see her eldest sister, who still lived there. In conversation she had asked her sister why it was that at times she had been called by her middle name.

Her sister had retorted, "Well, that's your name—that's what is on your birth certificate." Janet said she had never seen her real birth certificate—it had been lost—and the only one she had was the one that illegitimate children had. Her sister said, "Well, that's what you are!" At this point her sister angrily got up, left the room, and returned with Janet's birth certificate, which she thrust at her, saying, "There—read it!" Janet looked at the certificate and saw that the names given as her parents were not those of the people who had brought her up.

Janet was shocked and disbelieving. When she said this to her sister, her sister angrily told her that she had known about this—a childhood friend had told her when she was a little girl. Janet insisted she had never known that her parents were not her "real" parents. She then learned from her sister that she had been adopted at seven weeks. The person she had known as her father had been her uncle, her natural father's brother. When Janet read the name of her natural mother, she did not recognize the name. Her sister told her that she was the woman Janet knew as "Auntie Margaret". (In order to avoid confusion, from this point on I will refer to Janet's adoptive mother as her "mother" and to her natural mother as "Auntie Margaret".)

At that point Janet's sister realized that Janet had not consciously known about her birth. She became frightened about what she had done by telling Janet and told Janet's husband that she had thought she had known. She later acknowledged, however, that she had always believed that Janet should be told the truth; she felt that the deception had been at the root of Janet's problems when she was a child and young woman, and was the reason for her repeated breakdowns following her mother's death. Her parents had given Janet's birth certificate to her elder sister's husband, but he had been unable to tell her the truth about her birth, and, as her sister angrily said, "I was left to do it!"

Traumatized as she was when she related this to me, Janet said that when she saw the birth certificate, something clicked into place, and she suddenly discovered who she was.

I felt stunned by what I was being told.

Events in Janet's life gradually began to make sense to her. She recalled having been terrified when her mother once threatened to send her to the "cottage homes" if she didn't behave herself. She remembered asking her mother why it was that she, but not her sisters, went on weekly outings with Auntie Margaret, and being told that Margaret was lonely. She also recalled Auntie Margaret telling her to remember that two children she played with when she visited her were her cousins. As Janet couldn't make sense of this communication, she thought one of them must be mad. Now she saw that Auntie Margaret had been trying to tell her that she was her mother.

She knew that as a young child she had often experienced acute confusion and had then always curled up in the foetal position in a chair in the kitchen and gone to sleep. She remembered the first time she had experienced despair. It had occurred when she was 13 years old, and she had been unable to understand what was going on around her and had concluded that she must be mad. She remembered comforting herself with the thought that if she could not stand it any longer and could not carry on, she could always kill herself.

In "Adopted Children in Adolescence", Winnicott writes:

> The adolescent needs to find out about the real world, and that important part of the real world which revolves about the

general enrichment of relationships by instinct. Adopted children need this especially, because they feel insecure about their own origin. . . . Almost anything is of value if it is factual, and by the time a child gets near to a breakdown the need is so urgent that even unpleasant facts can be a relief. The trouble is *mystery*, and the consequent admixture of fantasy and fact, and the child's burden of the potential emotion of love, anger, horror, disgust, which is always in the offing but which can never be experienced. If the emotion is not experienced it can never be left behind. [Winnicott, 1955a, pp. 141–142]

Later in the paper, he says:

Children have an uncanny way of getting to know the facts eventually, and if they find that the person they have trusted has misled them, that matters to them far more than what they have discovered. [Winnicott, 1955a, p. 146]

Not surprisingly, for many months following this revelation from her sister, Janet was traumatized. Not only were her parents not her parents, but she was also illegitimate. In addition, she became alienated from her sisters. She felt furious, rejected, confused, and frightened, and in the therapy she regressed dramatically. She was brought to and collected from her sessions by her husband—she had handed over her "caretaker function" to him and to me (Winnicott, 1960b). After some months we agreed to increase her sessions to four times a week and later to five times. Whereas previously she had been immaculately dressed and made up (wearing the uniform and mask she had donned following her mother's death), she now came to sessions in sports shoes and socks and what she began calling "my rompers". These were pastel-coloured velour suits that did, in fact, resemble romper suits.

For a long time she and I occupied what Winnicott, writing about transitional phenonema, refers to as "neutral territory" (Winnicott, 1950, p. 143), "neutral area of experience" (Winnicott, 1951, p. 239) and "neutral zone" (Winnicott, 1971a, p. 64). In "Playing, Creative Activity and the Search for the Self", he writes,

The searching can come only from desultory formless functioning, or perhaps from rudimentary playing, as if in a neutral zone. It is only here, in this unintegrated state of the personality, that that which we describe as creative can appear. This if reflected back, *but only if reflected back*, becomes part of the organized individual personality, and eventually this in summation makes the individual to be, to be found; and eventually enables himself or herself to postulate the existence of the self. [Winnicott, 1971a, p. 64]

Janet required me to be there, not as an interpreting therapist, but instead as a provider of a setting in which she could retrace the path of her life given the new understanding she now had.

Once she had begun to recover from her shock, she began a search to find out the details of her early life.

As all four of her parents had been dead for some years, Janet had no direct access to a parental figure who could tell her about herself. She resumed contact with her sisters and learned from them that her mother had lost a little girl infant shortly before she herself was born. Janet had been described as "almost dead" when she had entered their family at the age of seven weeks, and the milk of one particular cow had been saved for feeding her. As for her natural father, she learned that he had made regular financial contributions to her parents for her keep and that he had ended his days in a mental institution. Her natural mother, Auntie Margaret, had moved in with her own sister and her family when her sister was ill and, following her sister's death, had married her husband and raised his children. These children were the ones she had tried to tell Janet were her cousins.

Janet's sister reminded her that, when she had been at the point of leaving the therapeutic community, she had planned to go to what was then Somerset House to look up their family tree. At that time her sisters were very frightened of her finding out the truth about her origins. When her elder sister told her of her birth, she believed Janet was pretending not to know and thought she had learned the truth when she went to Somerset House.

While Janet was engaged in her conscious search to find out about her roots, she was also unconsciously motivated to learn details about *my* life. I was a live human being—not dead, like her parents—but the details of my life were a mystery to her. Her curiosity about me was exceptional, and was unconsciously motivated by her desperation for me not to be a mysterious figure to her. At the time I experienced her behaviour as exceedingly intrusive.

The post sometimes arrived during Janet's sessions and was lying on the mat when she left. By scrutinizing the post, she discovered a number of things about my life. I frequently received post from abroad from a woman with an unsteady handwriting and a surname that was the same as the middle name that appeared on some of my letters. Janet rightly deduced that this person must be my mother. On one occasion she asked me whether she could have a magazine contained in a piece of post. On another occasion, when another middle name appeared on a letter, she became furious and demanded to know just how many names I had!

At this point Janet was beginning to be able to be angry in the present, and my middle name enabled her to express anger she had been unable to express in relation to her own middle name—the very thing that had provided the occasion for her to learn about her birth.

As I have already said, for a very long time Janet was brought to and collected from her sessions by her husband. One morning they arrived very early and were waiting outside when my husband and I returned from our morning walk. I recognized the car from some distance as we approached it and felt very awkward and embarrassed to be seen outside my house in my grubby clothes (as opposed to my work uniform) and decided simply to walk past the car without acknowledging Janet. This action was in keeping with my theoretical understanding at the time of maintaining a boundary around the session, but in ordinary human terms it was unnatural and impolite, and Janet felt confused and deeply hurt that I had not acknowledged her presence and greeted her.

When I had walked past as though I had not seen her, I had behaved falsely, and I am sure my manner conveyed that. Had I genuinely not seen her, my manner would have been different. When she came into her session angry that I had not acknowledged her, I interpreted that she was angry with me for appearing outside at a time when she had not expected to see me. Quite rightly, she refused to accept this interpretation compliantly and pressed me to tell her why I had not greeted her. It was only when I eventually admitted to her truthfully that I had seen her and had felt awkward and embarrassed that she was able to calm down.

This event signalled a turning-point in Janet's treatment. She had accurately sensed inauthenticity in me, been angry about it, demanded that I admit to it, and, furthermore, that I explain it to her. Up until then she had been prepared to accept my neutrality, although from time to time she had tried to move me from that stance in subtle ways. A further consequence of this confrontation was that it produced a shift in the transference. She no longer had me merged with her and therefore within her omnipotent control but was forced to regard me as a person in my own right, with my own awkwardness and embarrassment. In Winnicott's terms, I had become an object that could be used (Winnicott, 1971a).

Balint writes as follows of the difficulties in working with the regressed patient:

> True, the analyst must be prepared for some testing times, especially with regard to his sincerity. What these patients cannot tolerate is not receiving the truth, the whole truth, and nothing but the truth from their analyst. As a rule they are hypersensitive anyhow; they may react with pain and withdrawal to any show of insincerity, even to one which is comprised under the general heading of conventional forms of good manners. [M. Balint, 1968, p. 187]

In the transference I had become the deceitful mother, and in reality I could not be trusted. Janet's behaviour indicated she was frightened of me. She would go up the stairs to the consulting-room in what appeared to be quite a paranoid way—slightly sideways, with her head turned in a way that I experienced as letting me know she was keeping an eye on me. She became convinced that her mother had only taken her in for the money paid to her by Janet's natural father. And she believed that I only saw her "for the money". Presumably, she was sensitive to how difficult and demanding I was finding her at the time.

In spite of finding Janet's intrusive behaviour demanding, my countertransference was on the whole a positive one, and it alerted me to the special relationship Janet had had with her mother. I found her an extremely rewarding patient to work with, and I saw her at a time when I would not normally agree to see a patient. But at that time she had no awareness of being "special" to me. She later learned from a family friend that when her mother was in hospital, she had said to the friend that Janet was her favourite daughter.

Janet continued frequently to search me and my face when I opened the door to her and when she left her sessions. One Monday morning when she was putting on her coat at the end of her session, she commented that I looked tired. I spontaneously replied that I had been up late watching the Superbowl. This piece of information did not excite her curiosity as it might have done previously, and it did not lead to further questioning or a discussion about sport. Instead, it seemed to please her. It confirmed her ability to perceive my state accurately and enabled her to believe that I could be relied on to tell her the truth.

Although she may well not even remember this event, I recall it vividly. I realized after she had gone that I had surprised myself—responding with a piece of my own reality like this was not something I did. This acknowledgement on my part could be put down to the fact that I had stayed up late and was in fact tired, but it struck me at the time as an indicator that I no longer experienced Janet in the intrusive way that I had done previously. And what interested me subsequently was that her intrusive questioning and searching lessened as I was more prepared to give her the occasional piece of information—for example, at times I let her know where I would be during the breaks.

Some months ago Janet decided she wanted to have a small room built on to the side of their house. She had often complained in the past about not getting the sun in her garden because of neighbours' trees, but this room was to be built in a sunny spot and was to be "her room". She decided she would take her time over choosing not only the furnishings but also what type of floor and windows she wanted.

She then had the following dream:

They were having the room built onto the house except that a pre-fab room came and was put straight onto the house. It was very quick. The room was brick. Then she thought it was York stone or some-

thing—she didn't like it. Then when she looked at it again, it was glass.

Janet said that when she woke up she was in a muddle and could not think about the dream—but now that she was in her session, she could. She thought it related to the fact that she had been a pre-fab baby for her mother—a replacement baby for the one her mother had lost a short time before her birth. She did not want her room to be a quick, pre-fab room—she wanted it to be one that evolved over time, as she had done during her treatment. Her association to the fabric of the walls being glass was that she was reminded of a glass tray her mother had had on the wall; we had discussed it some months previously. At the time, we had come to understand the tray as a point of Janet's separation from her mother, as her mother had liked the tray and Janet had not. She had surprised herself by realizing that she was no longer merged in her mind with her mother, as she could see that they were two separate people with different tastes.

I understood the room to be a symbolic expression of Janet's true self as well as a replacement room for my consulting-room which she was creating for herself in anticipation of separating from me. Previously, when there had been re-decorating to be done, Janet had shopped around for the best bargain in a some-what obsessional way. When she had finally settled on something, inevitably she had been unhappy with it and had often com-plained to the place where she had purchased it. In contrast, it was gratifying to hear about the evolution of "her room" and the pleasure she was experiencing at each stage. Symbolically, she was no longer coming up against the various kinds of brick walls of her dream but was saying that her vision had become clearer—like the glass.

Some time before the Christmas break, Janet arrived at a ses-sion and playfully asked the question, "Who am I today?" She said she wanted to sit in the chair, and as she sat down she re-called having sat in that same position some years earlier. She said that she was sane for the first time in her life, and that that made her angry as she was faced with the idea of finishing her therapy and leaving me.

This account would not be complete without including the most recent event, which demonstrates another temporary movement on my part away from the stance of analytic neutrality—this event concerns the death of my own mother.

At the time of my mother's death, Janet was away on holiday with her husband and a group of his ex-colleagues and their wives. My mother's health had been gradually deteriorating for two years, and she died just over three weeks before the Easter break. I planned to go to the States on the Thursday for her funeral, return to work on the Monday afternoon, and then work until the break, when I could then return to the States. I knew that when Janet returned on Monday I only had two sessions in which either to cancel two of her sessions or to offer her a change of session times.

Janet returned from her holiday and, as she came in, growled playfully at me as though she were angry and said, "I'm just not ready to deal with people. It's your fault for encouraging me to go!" She spent the session recounting events from her holiday, including difficulties she had had with her friends, and bringing me up to date with where she was. At the end of that session I told her that I had a problem with her Thursday and Monday sessions and that we could either cancel them or I would try to offer her alternative times. As she went out, she said she wanted to know why I had a problem. I said that we could talk about it on Tuesday when we had more time.

The following day, when Janet came in, she was quite disoriented. She hung her coat up downstairs and left her umbrella there—thinking, it emerged later, that she was already in the consulting-room. She began by saying she wondered why I had a problem with the sessions. I had had her sessions to myself for the past two weeks, and now I had a problem with two of them.

I asked for her associations to this, and she said all she could think of was either that I had given them to someone else in her absence or that it was my way of getting rid of her and that I was rejecting her. She said I had never cancelled sessions before, and she had just come back and now I wanted to cancel two. After a while she remembered an occasion when I had cancelled a session. At this point I could see no point in teasing or tantalizing her—which I believed I would have been doing had I continued to remain an enigma.

I said that I believed she was again having difficulty in separating us and in seeing us as two separate people. She thought for a few minutes and then said she hoped nothing had happened to me. She became concerned and said she did not know how curious she could be.

I said, "And I do not know how much I can tell you without burdening you."

She immediately replied that she had spent all her life being protected from the truth, and she did not want that any more. Life was full of painful situations, and she did not want to go through any more of her life avoiding them.

She thought for a while and then said, "Your mother hasn't died, has she?"

I said that she had.

She wept and asked whether it was sudden.

I told her about my mother's failing health over the past two years and of her eventual death. Of course this was extremely painful for both of us, and we were both tearful, but in the circumstances it seemed the only honest and natural thing for me to do. She asked me questions about the circumstances, which I did not find in the least bit intrusive. She thanked me for telling her and said it was the first time anyone had ever been honest with her and not hidden something from her—it was the first time she had been treated as an adult. She then said that she did not need her sessions on those two days—that she felt she was helping me by not having them and that she would be all right. She said for me to have as much time off as was necessary. I said that I was planning to return for work late Monday afternoon, and that I felt that I would see her on Tuesday but that I would ring her on Monday when I got back.

On my return I telephoned her, and we arranged to meet on the Tuesday.

She came to the session with a beautiful plant for me. She sat up for some time while we talked about the funeral. She then lay on the couch and resumed talking about her difficulties with her friends on the holiday. After some time she stopped herself and said she was angry with herself because she was thinking about this when my mother had just died.

I said that I had burdened her.

She said in an exasperated tone, "But don't you see that I have always had the truth hidden from me. Don't you see what you have given me?"

I said that I could appreciate that. At the end of the session when she got up to go I thanked her for the plant and said how comforting it was.

During her Thursday session she resumed talking about the difficulties with her friends and her need to confront them. When she got up to go, she looked at me and said she was looking to see whether I was tired. I asked, "Am I?" She said, "Yes, you still don't look right." I said I supposed it would be strange if I did, and she agreed.

By the time the break arrived, Janet had confronted her friends with the behaviour that had upset her, and the crisis with them had passed and has not been mentioned since. What has been striking is that she has been able to talk about things that in the past would have caused her to lapse into depression, whereas recently she has become tearful but has then been able to move on to think about another area of her life.

At this point I want to look at why I involved Janet in details about my personal life when orthodox practice demands the reverse for the protection of the patient.

First of all, it seems reasonable to assume that conditions existed in Janet's infancy that approximate those described by Winnicott as producing a "False Self". Her sister's description of her as "almost dead" conjures up the picture of a baby whose mother was not "good-enough" (Winnicott, 1960b). Her reaction to her husband's reminder of their two boys who needed her suggests a mode of living with which she was already familiar. Certainly I had sensed an eagerness on her part to comply with me from the start, coupled with a fear of rejection if she did not.

It would appear that Janet was able to maintain a false self until the death of her mother. At that point, her original trauma of having been abandoned was re-experienced and her true, vulnerable self revealed, thereby exposing her false self. Her husband's reminder quickly enabled her to re-instate her false self, but without her mother there to strengthen it, it failed repeatedly over a period of more than twenty years. When she began intensive treatment with me, her true, vulnerable self became revealed once again via the re-enactment of the abandonment that she had experienced as a result of the break in treatment at six weeks. During that break Janet found a means of discovering her true origins.

On the final page of *New Foundations for Psychoanalysis*, when writing about the end of treatment, Laplanche says that the end "cannot mean the 'resolution of transference' because transference is a relationship with the enigmatic object" (Laplanche, 1989, p. 164).

I believe it is precisely because Janet lived so many years of her life with "enigmatic objects" that the finding of her true self was dependent upon her relationship with me as a "real object". If what she was faced with when she looked into her mother's eyes was an enigma, surely she herself could only be an enigma, as she had to keep hidden all of the countless things that she was unable to understand.

When she learned the details about her birth at the beginning of her treatment, I asked her permission to tell my colleague who had referred her. He immediately replied that she suddenly made sense to him—he had never been able to understand how or why she had ended up at the therapeutic community or what her treatment there had meant.

I am not disputing the fact that for the majority of patients analytic neutrality is not only valuable but necessary, as it was for Janet for much of the time. Before the Christmas break I had another patient say to me that she was very curious to know what I would be doing over the break, but she did not want to know as she did not want to see me as a person. For her at that time I was certainly required to remain neutral.

I cannot deny that Janet represents an extreme example of a false self. She spent 57 years of her life in a state of confusion, not knowing who she was but believing herself to be mad, as her feelings were inexplicable to her. My work with her has caused me to question the viability of maintaining a stance of analytic neutrality with patients whose presenting problem is of the false self variety.

As she emerges from her depression and grief and leaves behind her false compliant self, Janet exhibits a vivacious, lively, and fun-loving personality. Apart from "her room", she has found another venue for the expression of her true self. This is in the stands of the local Premier League football team, where she, her husband, their eldest son, and his young son are season ticket holders. Another obvious signal that she is moving away from me, and that we have embarked on the final phase of her therapy, occurred recently, when Janet asked for a change of session time. When I offered her an evening time, she quickly replied without thinking that she was not sure that she could make that time, as her team might be playing that evening. Far from experiencing this as an attack on either me or the therapy, this was a moment of pure enjoyment between us, as for once another activity had taken precedence over her therapy session.

Harry Guntrip wrote movingly about his analytic experiences with Fairbairn and Winnicott and ended his account with this statement:

> All through life we take into ourselves both good and bad figures who either strengthen or disturb us, and it is the same in psychoanalytic therapy: it is the meeting and interacting of two real people in all its complex possibilities. [Guntrip, 1975, p. 156]

For 99.9% of the many hours that Janet and I have spent in each other's company, I have sat in my chair, she has lain on the couch, and together we have tried to make sense of her past and her present, both in her relationship with me and in her relationships with her family members, friends, and others in the outside world. Our work together has been ordinary psychotherapeutic work, and for the most part one would struggle to find something exceptional in either the material she has brought or in the interpretations I have made. Having said that, however, our work has repeatedly been brought into sharp relief by the extraordinary fact that until the beginning of her treatment she literally did not know who she was or whose she was.

Without the 99.9% there could, of course, be no .1%. What has happened in that .1% has been most crucial, however, in that it has been in those moments that we have made direct contact as two ordinary human beings, and those moments have, I believe, helped to enable Janet to find her true self. In those moments it has been demanded of me that I be my true self—my real self—and not an enigmatic therapist.

CHAPTER TWO

The concept of internal cohabitation

Joscelyn Richards

To be an effective psychoanalytic psychotherapist, it is essential to develop a theoretical framework or model that is personally valid and based on a thorough understanding of psychoanalytic theory. This framework will be modified to incorporate repeated and careful observations from personal analysis and clinical work with patients.

Writing this chapter presents me with an opportunity to describe a conceptualization of mental life that I have been working with and developing with colleagues for approximately the last ten years. The concept is one of "internal cohabitation" or "coresidency" of two selves or egos in the one body, and was developed by Michael Sinason, with the help of myself and other colleagues (Sinason, 1993). The concept of internal cohabitation emerged from a clinical workshop for psychoanalytic psychotherapists working with patients diagnosed as having a manic-depressive illness and involves a dual-track analysis of two co-existing selves, each of whom has a mind of their own.

I began to take an interest in the concept of internal cohabitation when I found that existing theories did not satisfactorily explain certain phenomena that I had become increasingly aware of in my psychoanalytic psychotherapy with patients. In particular, I experienced an impasse with a number of patients who showed genuine motivation for insight and change but then behaved as if these had never been desired.

The opposition to the therapeutic dyad

With several patients I had the dislocating experience that the person I was with last session—or even two minutes, or seconds, ago—had gone and been replaced by another person with the same face, body, and clothes but whose whole demeanour, facial expression, tone of voice, and language were different. One moment there was a capacity and interest in appraising our interactions and a perception of me as a helpful partner, whilst the next there was resentment of the whole therapeutic enterprise, a wish to obstruct it at every turn, and behaviour suggesting attitudes of suspicion, antagonism, superiority, or indifference towards me as the therapist. There was either hostility or a pseudo-cooperation at any attempt to explore the basis of these changes.

A female patient who at one moment was exploring with me in an involved manner the reasons why there had been difficulties between sessions in remembering the help I had given her was, in the next moment, looking away from me and saying in a brittle, impatient voice that it was time to end her therapy. A male patient who was in three-times-a-week psychotherapy had two very good consecutive sessions in which we were able to explore certain aspects of his inner world. Then he arrived at the third session looking tense and guarded. When I referred to something I remembered him saying in the previous session, he looked at me in disgust and said, "I don't know who you're talking about ... you're speaking absolute drivel. I don't know anything about that". As I opened my mouth to speak, the patient put his hands over his ears and said: "I can't hear you." In some ways I deserved this scoffing dismissal, as I had not used my observation of the tense, guarded appearance of the patient to inform myself that something had changed.

I often observed that patients treated me as if I were dangerous, hypocritical, or useless and reacted accordingly with fear,
hostility, or contempt. Whatever I then said was received by the
patient as confirmation of this denigratory view of me as the
therapist. The pressures in the patient to perceive me as malign or
ineffectual, and the pressures in me to take on the projection,
could be subtle or overt but were nearly always very effective.
When these pressures were operative, I could feel myself in the
grip of a process that was relentlessly pushing me to match the
patient's expectations.

Patients themselves expressed awareness of alternating experiences. The male patient mentioned above was late for an early
morning session and said: "I don't know what happened . . . I got
up at the right time and the next thing I knew it was past the time
to leave . . . someone must have altered the clock." This same patient described how whole chunks of time disappeared and how
he would suddenly "come to" and realize that time had passed
and then feel that someone else had been directing his life. Thus
he felt that he had been living in an army parade-ground and had
been marching about under orders from a "sergeant-major" who
threatened dire consequences if he did not "toe the line". Patients
often communicated that this experience of being taken over was
completely outside their control. For example, after a tense ten-
minute silence, a patient said tearfully, "I was sure I'd be able to
speak to you today . . . I don't understand what happens, it's like
something steps in . . . I don't want to be like this". Another patient spoke of "something alien which is forced into me and I
don't want it—the way I behave is monstrous".

Patients also seemed to be pointing to an undermining, sabotaging process over which they had no control when they commented on patterns they had become aware of: "Just as everything
feels all right, it all goes wrong again", or, "as soon as I begin to
feel hopeful, something happens to make me get depressed
again". A patient of a therapist I have supervised spoke of "terrible setbacks" and "terrible pains" that invaded his body just as
he was feeling well again.

Often, however, it was very difficult for patients to see these
patterns because there seemed to be an internal activity that
wiped out memories as well as the capacity to think and make

connections. Patients frequently commenced sessions by announcing that they were trying to remember the last session but were unable to do so, or during a session a patient would go blank in the middle of saying something important. Sometimes patients were overcome with sleepy feelings as soon as anything to do with the relationship with me was mentioned. They had various ways of letting me know that they could not help or control these "take-overs" of their sensory, motor, and perceptual apparatus. They tried to convey that they wanted to stay in communication with me as well as carry out the plans and hopes they had for themselves but felt helpless, imprisoned, and frightened by the powerful processes that drove them to do the opposite of what they wished to say or do. Some patients felt so overwhelmed by these forces that they gave up having any plans. For example, an overweight patient said that she would like to participate in the sponsored weight loss organized by her church, "but it would be no good joining in because the converse side of myself will insist on doing the opposite". Another patient said she could never work out what she thinks and feels because "the other side is always jumping in accusing me of having no right to my feelings . . . when I try to present my views a voice from nowhere says 'Oh listen to you'". This sneering voice, which endlessly criticized her for trying to take herself seriously, could make her feel so confused and undermined that she would feel like throwing herself under a bus.

It often seemed that patients had the recurring experience of another self, one different from the one who arrived at the session, taking over the minute the session started and behaving, as one patient put it, "in a bloody-minded way" that was the opposite of what they had intended. There was then a fear that the therapist would not be interested in understanding this phenomenon but would assume that the patient had control over what was happening and that the "bloody-mindedness" and rejection of the therapist would be misunderstood. As one of my patients said: "I really worry about your reaction—I think to myself Miss Richards will think I don't want to see her any more and will tell me to shove off and not return. When I really think about it I know you're not the sort of person who would do that but at the time I think you probably will. Sometimes I am sure you are going to."

Conceptual issues

When I first started observing and experiencing these dislocating phenomena, I was not sure what conceptualizations to employ to make sense of them. Initially I thought the sudden change towards the therapist and the therapeutic exploration was a negative therapeutic reaction due to innate destructiveness or hatred of dependence, or a reaction to a wrong or insensitive interpretation on my part. I understood the patient's bewilderment to be the result of mechanisms of splitting and projection or those of denial and disavowal. It seemed that the ego or self disowned or split off unwanted parts or feelings. Thus, I would think of the patient as disowning his destructiveness or his hatred of me or the therapy, and that the purpose of the therapy was to help him recognize and own these aspects.

However, there was something about the bewilderment and distress of patients who felt driven to think, feel, and see things in ways that later—or even concurrently—did not make sense to them that led me to consider that these concepts did not do justice to their experience. Alternative concepts, such as the re-emergence of repressed memories or perverse internalized object relationships, were also unsatisfactory, as they did not fit with the histories of these patients or with the range of situations and interactions where these experiences of being taken over occurred. I therefore came to the conclusion that I would have to take seriously the patients' statements that they experienced themselves as being in two minds or being two people with different perceptions and attitudes.

It meant taking seriously, for example, a patient who responded to my comment that she was always feeling torn between two points of view as to what sort of person she was by saying, "I am two people". She then spoke of the difficulty of living with this inner division: "Most people don't see two sides, they only see one—it feels ridiculous to say to someone, 'I've got this other person', it sounds bizarre, schizophrenic". Acknowledging this, however, seemed to give her much relief and led to her exploring and illustrating how she could not do or think anything without feeling sneered at and told off by someone else inside her head.

It also meant taking seriously my repeated observations that this supposedly split-off subordinate part was, in fact, behaving like an independent person and objecting, often strongly, either to the patient's plans or to the working alliance established between therapist and patient. I had particularly noticed that patients often used a language that implied that a part was perceived to have a personal motive—for example, the patient who said ". . . the converse side . . . *will insist* . . ." or the patient who said, ". . . the other side *is always jumping in accusing me of having no right to my feelings* . . .". In addition, this part, rather than being subordinate, often behaved like *the senior partner*—for example, the patient who explained that he had felt driven all his life by someone in his head who gave orders like a sergeant-major; or the patient who said "this part of me seems to have a mind of its own". The concept of first ego-splitting and then employing a range of defences to deal with the splits was insufficient to explain the range of phenomena in which I had become interested.

It was my psychotherapeutic work for many years with a manic-depressive patient that particularly led me to question the concepts I was using. We had reached something of an impasse, and initially I thought that the difficulties were due to my inadequacies as a therapist and/or the severity of the patient's pathology; but gradually I had begun to think that they might be due more to the inadequacies of my conceptual framework. The concept of "internal cohabitation" or the "co-residency" of two minds in one body offered a useful alternative to the concepts of splitting, disavowal, or perverse internalized objects. To move from these familiar concepts to that of internal cohabitation seemed initially a large step. However, an examination of the literature indicated that many clinicians in the psychoanalytic field have accepted the possibility of more than one internal agency (Grotstein, 1985; Rowan, 1990) whilst others have struggled to make sense of clinical material that points to the possibility of a patient's intentions and autonomy being taken over by another mind (Sinason, 1993).

In his early studies in hysteria, Freud, along with Breuer, came to the ". . . bewildering realisation that in one and the same individual there can be several mental groupings, which can 'know nothing' of one another and which can alternate with one another in their hold upon consciousness" (Freud, 1910a, p. 19). This observation was first made in relation to hypnotic phenomena, but Freud went on to describe a duality that occurred "spontaneously", which he called a "double conscience" (Freud, 1910a). Breuer was even more explicit, and in describing his first analytic patient, Anna O, he wrote, "Two entirely distinct states of consciousness were present which alternated very frequently and without warning and which became more and more differentiated in the course of the illness" (Breuer, in Freud, 1895d, p. 24). "It is hard to avoid expressing the situation by saying that the patient was split into two personalities of which one was mentally normal and the other insane" (Breuer, in Freud, 1895d, p. 45).

For many years Freud developed the concept of repression, seeing this as the primary mechanism of defence of the ego in his structural model of the mind. Nevertheless, he remained interested in the possibility of the ego "effecting a cleavage or division of itself" (Freud, 1924b [1923], pp. 152–153). He returned more fully to the phenomenon of two states of mind in his work on fetishism (Freud, 1927e), where he developed the concept of disavowal. He finally concluded, near the end of his working life, that the splitting into two contradictory states of mind, one normal and the other abnormal, was not only a feature of fetishism but also of the psychoses and neuroses:

> One learns from patients after their recovery [from psychosis] that at the time in some corner of their mind (as they put it) there was a normal person hidden, who, like a detached spectator watched the hubbub of illness go past him. . . . We may probably take it as being generally true that what occurs in all these cases is a psychical *split*. Two psychical attitudes have been formed instead of a single one—one, the normal one, which takes account of reality, and another which, under the influence of the instincts, detaches the ego from reality. The two exist alongside of each other. [Freud, 1940a (1938), p. 202]

The extension of the frontiers of psychoanalysis to working with borderline, narcissistic, and psychotic patients has particularly contributed to awareness of different modes of mental functioning that are perceived either to co-exist or to alternate within the one human body. Following Bion's description of the importance of differentiating the psychotic personality from the non-psychotic personality (Bion, 1957), a great deal of work has been put into understanding and describing the major characteristics of the psychotic state of mind or personality and the importance for clinicians in recognizing the psychotic wavelength (Lucas, 1992).

As a result of this work, there is probably considerable agreement amongst many clinicians on the major characteristics of the psychotic personality—for example:

• hatred of reality, thinking, and dependence;

• the conviction that all relationships are exploitative and that creative intercourse (literally and metaphorically) cannot exist;

• extreme narcissistic sensitivity;

• concrete, absolutist and rigid thinking;

• the replacement of symbolic functioning by the use of symbolic equations. Segal (1981) has written extensively on the concept of symbolic equation in which the psychotic mind cannot truly symbolize but sees two things that have some aspects in common as being literally the same;

• an incapacity to learn from experience.

There is agreement also that the non-psychotic personality can learn from experience, can think, can symbolize and make associations and connections, enjoys the mutuality of relationships, and has the capacity and desire to make differentiations and to recognize and negotiate internal and external reality. There may also be agreement with the view of Freud, Klein, Bion, and Rosenfeld that there is a psychotic aspect in all human beings, even though the extent and influence varies. Bion also thought that patients who are overtly psychotic have a non-psychotic or neurotic personality (Bion, 1957).

Grotstein (1985), amongst others, suggests that the concept of the splitting of the ego has been most likely to lead to an understanding of the phenomenon of different modes of functioning occurring in the same human being. This has been the case whether the splitting has been conceptualized as being due to an unmanageable death instinct (Klein, 1948) or to an inevitable failure of maternal provision (Fairbairn, 1952), or to both. It seems as if clinicians can find it very helpful to make a differentiation between two very different states of mind but hold back from conceptualizing separate personality structures from birth. For example, Grotstein writes of "separate selves having different agendas, scenarios and motivations" but conceptualizes the separateness as being due to "dissociative phenomena" (Grotstein, 1985, p. 68), and Rowan writes of "a *sub*-personality [as]a semi-permanent and semi-autonomous region of the personality capable of acting as a person" (Rowan, 1990, p. 8). Roth (1988) illustrates the usefulness, in helping to resolve an impasse, of recognizing the existence of two parts that are so split from each other that they operate very differently in the analytic situation and have very different attitudes towards the analyst. She thus speaks to the parts as if they were two persons who need to be differentiated from each other. However, in her discussion she does not raise the possibility of conceptualizing the parts as separate personalities, even though the clinical material invites the possibility. I am not sure of the reasons for this reluctance. It may have to do with an anxiety—which I have certainly experienced myself at times—of challenging the more usual concepts of splitting and of one ego in one body, even though the concept of two egos in one body from birth on seems to me to be a further development of, rather than a radical departure from, previous models that recognize the co-existence of different modes of apprehending reality.

The authors who have particularly influenced me in their attempt to address conceptually the clinical phenomena pointing to the possibility of separate and autonomous personalities have been the post-Kleinians, Bion and Rosenfeld. They both observed that there seemed to be an ill personality that could dominate and intimidate the sane patient. Rosenfeld, particularly, developed, in the latter part of his life, his concept of "the narcissistic omnipotent self", which adopts bully tactics when that self feels threatened by the libidinal self's relationship with the therapist. In his final book (1987), published posthumously, he describes the problems "the narcissistic omnipotent self" creates for the patient who is attempting to understand his/her difficulties in sustaining attachments, especially as they are manifest in the relationship with the psychotherapist. In his view this self secretly influences and imprisons the "libidinal self" and, in order to retain dominance, attempts to prevent the patient from forming and sustaining a working relationship with the therapist. Rosenfeld thought that the "narcissistic omnipotent self" changes from being seductive and persuasive to being denigrating and belittling of the patient as his capacities for understanding and relating develop.

However, neither Bion's nor Rosenfeld's conceptualization of separate personalities was completely consistent. For example, Bion sometimes spoke of parts and Rosenfeld sometimes described the narcissistic omnipotent self as a phantasy and a projection of the ego. Also, neither seemed to consider addressing the need to have a concern for the plight of the ill self caused by the analytic situation.

Amongst Independent psychoanalysts, Winnicott, with his concept of the true and false selves, was also attempting to find an explanation for the observation of an internal agency that presents itself as the main or sole self or agent when there is clinical evidence of another self. Winnicott's view that the main function of the false self is to be a caretaker of the true self provided some basis for explaining the attacks on the therapy and the therapy couple when there is a perception of the therapist attacking (through impingement) the true self. His view also helped me to have empathy for a patient's need to be defensive. However, I did not find that the concept of the false or caretaker self sufficiently explained the omnipotent and paranoid attacks on the therapy and the therapy couple when the healthy or true self had reached a stage of feeling genuinely held and understood by the therapist. Also, I found that the terminology could be confusing: although Winnicott intended the concept of false self to refer to an internal structure that decided that behaviour should be compliant rather than authentic (to protect the true self from traumatic impingement), the actual term "false self" can be misunderstood to mean "not real".

Fairbairn, too, was interested in psychic structures, their origins, and the conflicts within and between them. His concept of an internal saboteur—which he later redefined as the anti-libidinal ego that attacks the libidinal ego—seemed at first to provide a possible explanation for the attacks on the therapy. However, both the anti-libidinal and the libidinal egos are conceptualized as split off from a central, organizing ego due to environmental pressures. Fairbairn thus thought that the split between these two part-egos could be repaired through the processes of therapy.

In reviewing the clinical material for evidence that might resolve the matter of how to conceptualize the nature of the "other" mind, the choice seemed to be between one psychic structure at birth, which later splits, under inevitable external and/or internal pressures, into two or more parts, or two separate and autonomous psychic structures at birth, which are organized according to different aims and principles and hence perceive and react to reality in different ways. Even though I have found the latter conceptualization the most clinically useful, the issue is difficult to resolve, partly because, even with improved methods of infant observation and research, we cannot see directly into the minds of infants and partly because there can be different interpretations of the same behaviour.

The issue needs to be resolved, however, because of the consequences for understanding transference and countertransference phenomena and the nature of what constitutes a mutative interpretation. If there is one ego that splits into two—or three, as in Fairbairn's model—then the aim of psychoanalytic psychotherapy is to help the patient to experience and understand what has been split off and why. It also involves recognizing the damaging consequences of the split, understanding the methods and defences employed to maintain it, and, through these processes, bringing about the integration of the parts. If, however, there are two psychic structures from birth, characterized by different aims and mental functioning, then the aim of psychoanalytic psychotherapy is to help the patient to differentiate him/herself from the ill self (which may be representing him/herself as the senior partner and be in a very dominant position) by understanding the characteristics of this personality and what situations cause this one to become disturbed and why.

If there are two autonomous minds, then the attempt to understand them as split-off parts and to help integrate them back into the ego involves attributing to the sane person ambitions, perceptions, and motives that are not his but those of the disturbed personality. For example, paranoid, narcissistic, and retaliatory behaviour will be inaccurately attributed to the non-psychotic self, instead of being recognized as the ill personality's reactions to perceived criticism and denigration by both the sane patient and the psychotherapist. This may explain why some patients feel demoralized by their therapy and have a profound sense of being either bad or misunderstood or feel very confused about their identity.

Sinason addresses the conceptual and clinical issues by considering the identity of an inner, troublesome voice that everyone seems to experience, though in different ways. He examines the difficulties inherent in the previous attempts to account for this inner voice and proposes that the concept of internal cohabitation of two autonomous minds in one body from birth provides a framework for conducting a dual-track analysis in which neither mind is considered to be subsidiary to, nor split off from, the other (Sinason, 1993). He describes in this paper what he and colleagues observed again and again in their clinical work—namely, that only one mind is able to think and change. That mind can form a working alliance with the psychotherapist, whilst at the same time the other mind cannot learn from experience, is not able to change, and fears and hates being recognized. This other mind, therefore, perceives the psychotherapist and the working alliance only as a threat to his/her survival.

Since the publication of Sinason's paper (1993) a number of other papers have used the concept of internal cohabitation. Whilst it could not be argued that they conclusively prove the existence of two autonomous minds, they do illustrate the clinical usefulness of the concept and its applicability across a range of patients and issues. March (1997) found the concept useful in understanding why patients who had willingly agreed to carry out certain tasks as part of their cognitive behaviour therapy were then unable to do so. Bacelle (1993) found it useful to differentiate the two selves when analysing a patient with marked paranoid and psychotic views. In his paper he refers to Jung's interest in psychosis and his awareness of "two egos". Jenkins (1995) also found the concept of internal cohabitation very useful in working with psychotic patients and that patients "across the spectrum of diagnostic categories allude . . . to states of mind and emotion in which their autonomy is taken over to the detriment of their own goals and ambitions". He found that these patients are then helped to become less enmeshed with their ill self through analytic understanding of the autonomy and the characteristics of this internal "other self".

Since incorporating the concept into my own clinical work, I have found it useful in understanding a range of patients. It is my experience that, although internal cohabitation is most vividly observed in patients with a formal diagnosis of psychosis, and of borderline and narcissistic personality disorders, it occurs across all diagnostic categories, including patients with depressive and neurotic disorders. The precise nature of the internal relationship and the extent and frequency with which the psychotic personality dominates the other varies from patient to patient. I have found that the concept was of help particularly in understanding negative therapeutic reactions and in differentiating those that are a response to real progress from those that are a response to a poor interpretation (Richards, 1993). I have also found it useful for understanding the intrusion into a patient's mind of a recurring and urgent impulse to end the psychotherapy, even though she had expressed a strong desire to continue (Richards, 1994), and an overwhelming urge in another patient to sleep through many of her sessions, which deeply embarrassed her, and the occurrence of sleepy feelings in myself as the therapist (Richards, 1995).

During the past ten years, my work with patients and the supervision of other psychotherapists have led me to the conclusion that the concept of two autonomous minds co-existing since birth enables both patient and therapist to understand the opposition to the therapy and to the therapeutic dyad. If the therapist "forgets" that living internally with the patient is another mind, which feels threatened by the working alliance between the patient and therapist, then attacks on the psychotherapeutic work cannot be fully understood, and patients either get into a battle with this other mind (and/or the therapist) or remain entangled with him/her. However, if the therapist remembers the existence of the other mind, then patients can be helped to differentiate themselves from the convictions and misperceptions of their internal cohabitee and can develop a capacity to understand and look after him/her.

The following excerpt from a session of a male patient one year after starting in three-times-a-week therapy illustrates some of this therapeutic development:

"I think I've got clearer about the internal other person. After Wednesday's session I was able to see him more clearly and see what he's like: he's like a child that's got stuck . . . he can't see the implications of what he does, and he makes instant judgements and can't think he could be wrong. He needs me to be like a parent to him, but it's very difficult because it's not a simple matter of good and bad, like I thought . . . in fact I realize it's him that thinks that way. I, too, am insecure, and he can play on that. I have to be like a parent to him but he doesn't trust me . . . he never has. He always says I'm no good and up 'til now I've believed him. I have to take care of him and not abuse and criticize him and say he's mad. It wouldn't help a real child . . . and anyway he is real. He gets very frightened. He's like my father, who's paranoid. They both say you can't trust anyone and you have to go round expecting to be mugged. I'm only just realizing how much my life has been limited by that attitude."

Because I have so far found that the concept of internal cohabitation applies across all diagnostic categories, I have concluded that it is a universal condition and that therefore psychotherapists, too, have another, psychotic, mind that resides internally with them and has the potential to interfere with their capacity to understand and function appropriately as a therapist. Phenomena such as ending sessions early or late, falling asleep during them, making an interpretation that is later recognized to have been over-friendly or hostile are examples of therapists not being aware of take-overs by their internal cohabitee. Certainly, it has been useful and necessary for me to get to know and monitor the reactions of my internal cohabitant at all times in my analytic work. It is my experience—both directly with patients and through supervising other psychotherapists—that the patient's and the therapist's internal cohabitees can respond very quickly to each other, and recognition of this not only enables anticipation of situations that would otherwise become countertransference enactments (such as inappropriate or hostile interpretations) but helps the therapist in the task of understanding the patient's internal cohabitee (Richards, 1993, 1995). Thus, the concept of universal internal cohabitation brings a new, dual-track perspective to the task

of using the countertransference to understand the patient's transference.

Clinical illustration

Some of the features that occur in psychoanalytic psychotherapy
with manic–depressive patients also occur with other patients but
seem to be writ large with patients with a bipolar illness. These
features often cause particular difficulties for the therapist. For
example, the patient tends either to speak so fast that the therapist
feels flooded with information and ideas, or to have no thoughts
at all, helplessly waiting to be told what to do. In both situations,
the therapist can have considerable difficulty in thinking and can
feel pushed internally and externally to respond non-analytically.
In the first situation, there can be a desire to instruct the patient to
slow down or an urge to keep up with the pace and comment on
everything that has been said and thus join in or outdo the manic
behaviour. In the second situation, there can be a pressure to do
all the work—to give advice or ask questions in an attempt to get
the patient to speak—or, when there is no response, only a vacant
look, to switch off altogether. In both situations the therapist may
feel helpless as to how to engage with the patient in understanding what is happening when there seems to be no one there with
whom to think.

I will examine further the first situation—where the patient is
tending towards manic flight and pressure of talk—using the concept of internal cohabitation. Before doing so, however, I will
make some comments on my terminology.

In the course of developing the concept of internal cohabitation, it was difficult to decide what language to use, in discussions
both with colleagues and with patients. Bion's terminology, of
"psychotic and non-psychotic personalities", is useful conceptually but cannot be used directly with the patient as the term psychotic is experienced as an accusation of madness. Patients often
help by providing their own terms—for example, the "sergeant-
major" or "my other self". Sometimes the term has to be changed
when it begins to emerge that there is a problem with its use. For
example, with the patient I discuss below, we had referred for a

while to her cohabitee as a saboteur. The patient was happy with this term, as it identified the source of the opposition to her therapy, but her cohabitee began to react adversely, and we stopped using the term when we realized that her cohabitee felt maligned by being described as a saboteur. We also used the term the "ill one", but at the time of the session to be presented we were tending to say "the other one" as it seemed more neutral.

In the clinical illustration, I use the convention developed with my colleagues of referring to the sane personality as "the patient" and to the psychotic personality as "the cohabitee" or "cohabitant", when writing about them. When talking to the patient, I address her as "you"; when talking to her about her cohabitee, I say "she" or "the other one".

The patient

Ms J

At the time of the session Ms J was in her late forties and had a long history of manic–depressive breakdowns. She was usually admitted to hospital when overtaken by a manic state of mind because, if uncontained, it led her into dangerous and destructive situations and behaviour—for example, spending all her money, throwing away many of her needed possessions such as her handbag and her desk, with their contents, being sexually disinhibited, walking the streets at night, and so on. In this state she often had the belief that she had a direct line to God or that she was Jesus Christ. When depressed, she was usually not admitted to hospital but stayed at home in bed, contacting no one and not answering the door or the telephone. In this state she had made many suicide attempts, including cutting her wrists and throat. At these times there was a view that she was ugly, unwanted, and hated by everyone, combined with an equivalent hatred of everyone else.

Ms J had not been employed for many years but had worked quite successfully during her twenties and early thirties, though it had always been a strain. She is an intelligent woman, but since her first breakdown in her late twenties she had not been able to fulfil her potential. Her first breakdown occurred when she became engaged, and the engagement was subsequently broken off. For some years she had had a fairly stable relationship with a man about her own age, whom I call "Johnny" in the session, who had also had breakdowns and admissions to hospital quite often. They tended to support each other when ill and be appreciative of the other when well. However, negotiating an appropriate separateness from Johnny was often agonizing for Ms J because she could be taken over by a belief that separation meant rejection.

I had seen this patient for some years before working with the concept of internal cohabitation. The session I am going to present occurred nearly four years after I had started using the concept in my work with her. I had an opportunity, using this framework, to re-evaluate the behaviour I used to think of as belonging to Ms J: for example, a conviction of being abandoned between sessions, total hatred of the therapist for abandoning her, followed by complete denial of any need of the therapist, followed by desperate persuasion for the therapist to give concrete reassurance of caring about the patient, and so on. When making interpretations according to a one-ego model with split-off parts, Ms J did not find my transference interpretations helpful. In fact, she found them so unhelpful that I had to stop making them, and because of this we were considering bringing the therapy to an end.

However, changing the focus so that Ms J was helped to recognize the existence of another person who lived with her internally and who frequently took her over enabled Ms J to develop some capacity to recognize the intense paranoid convictions and the tram-lined mental functioning of her internal cohabitee and how these contributed to the development of psychotic depression and hypomania. At first Ms J found it difficult to make the change, but gradually she found the experience of differentiating herself from the internal co-habitant to be helpful. Separations between sessions and during holidays began to be possible without the patient being taken over by the cohabitee's hypomanic or depressive reactions. This was because Ms J began to recognize that the ill personality always perceived a break as a "chasm" into which she irretrievably fell or, worse, into which I gladly threw her. This enabled her to realize that, in contrast, she perceived a break as a "pause", which she likened both to a bridge and to the end of a chapter. However, this process of differentiation, which she found helpful, created difficulties for the cohabitee of her body, who vigorously opposed this new understanding, and this in turn created difficulties for the patient.

In the earlier therapy we talked about the patient being high or low, and the patient always felt that these mood swings occurred without rhyme or reason and were to do with biochemical changes over which she had absolutely no control and which had no personal meaning. The differentiation between the patient and her internal cohabitee enabled discovery of the reasons for these changes of mood.

At the time of the session to be presented, I was seeing Ms J three times a week, on Monday, Wednesday, and Friday. The session being presented occurred on a Friday. In the previous session Ms J had been able to differentiate herself from her cohabitee and then recognize how her internal cohabitee was disturbed by this process and by our relationship.

The session

Ms J was in the toilet when I went to collect her—she emerged about five minutes late. Whilst I was hovering between the consulting- and waiting-rooms—some yards from the ladies' toilet—I could hear the rustling of toilet paper. Whenever I had heard the rustling in the past, the patient had been in a manic state; thus I expected someone to emerge who would look in disarray and might make a seemingly flippant comment. I remembered that, in the past, before I understood that the voice in my head (from my internal cohabitee) could become competitive with the patient's cohabitee and resent her presence, I had often felt irritated at the patient's disturbed behaviour. A flicker of a frown would show on my face, by which the patient was understandably further disturbed. However, when she appeared, she looked herself and walked in a calm way to the consulting-room. Nevertheless, I held on to my thoughts about the possibility of her cohabitee and mine being actively present and influencing each other.

P: [*silence, then speaking fast*] I couldn't remember the last session. I've been pulled towards depression. . . . I've been fighting it—with the help of drugs, of course. . . . I'm on anti-depressants. . . . I can feel pulls towards going high but also low. I'm going up and down . . . [*She kept talking fast and in that vein*]

[*Pause* . . .]

T: I wonder if the other one who co-exists with you internally wants us to think in the old terms of high and low, but trying to remember the previous session indicates that you want to understand why she feels she has to rush through the session.

P: [*speaking at an ordinary pace*] I thought a lot about what you said in the Wednesday session—how she got frightened and worried about being abandoned because you and I—and not your ill one and my ill one—but you and I were able to communicate.

I was telling Johnny about it. We had a good evening—for the first time in ages we put on records and listened to music, and when it was time to go he left, and I had a bath. It wasn't mad playing of music, like other times when I'd stay up all night. Also, it felt all right for Johnny to leave. I think she feels left out of that relationship too—just like she feels left out of the one with you.

When I was having the bath, suddenly the thought came into my head—the grim reaper—it kept coming—the grim reaper. That's the personification of death—there was this image of the grim reaper. I thought it was her and not me having this image, but I didn't know why she kept having it. I thought, is she telling me to kill myself. I couldn't think why she would do that—but then I thought it was like you said—that she doesn't like me talking to you and Johnny—but that didn't quite make sense.

I was thinking about differentiating myself from her. . . . I could see they were her thoughts and not mine. . . . I think you were saying last session that when I differentiate myself from her, she feels she is going to be rejected.

[*Pause* . . .]

T: When you're thinking of her feeling rejected because you have differentiated yourself from her, I wonder if you are beginning to think that her thought, "the grim reaper", was not telling you to kill yourself but rather was her automatic reaction to you differentiating yourself from her—that is, she feels you are the grim reaper who is killing her when you enjoy talking to me and Johnny.

P: [*in an emphatic voice*] Why should she think differentiation has to mean killing her?

[*Pause . . . I felt internally pushed to answer but recognized this as my cohabitee's response and waited, and Ms J continued.*]

She seems to see differentiation as separation—I think of it more as me finding a space to be myself. I want to be my-self—I need to be myself—I do need to differentiate myself from her but [*speaking faster and faster*] she seems to feel it's like Siamese twins who are joined at the heart—if you sepa-rate them they die . . . it's horrible.

T: I think you are very interested in getting to recognize her and how she feels fatally wounded as you become clearer about yourself as a separate person, but she seems to be finding it so difficult that she is trying to rush you through the exploration and the session.

P: I am speeding aren't I . . . or she is.

[*Slowing down . . .*]

I think it does frighten her . . . how can I make her see that I'm not going to kill her—I'd have to kill myself if I killed her . . .

T: Because you have the same body.

P: Exactly. [*Pause . . .*] What do I *do* to make her see? She doesn't really learn—[*speaking fast again*] she can't change—that's horrible.

T: I wonder if she speaks fast because she can't bear you to pause and take your time in recognizing the impossibility of her changing. Someone keeps saying "that's horrible". I wonder if she thinks she is horrible because she can't change and she assumes you think she is horrible and must separate from her, which to her means cutting her off from you—that is, abandoning her.

P: I thought it was me thinking it was horrible for her to be always there thinking she is going to die—it is horrible. Well, what do I *do*?

T: As you start to think about the difficulties of her situation and yours—living with someone who feels sure she is going to die every time you differentiate yourself from her—she immediately feels her situation can only be thought of as horrible and takes over your language and assumes you've got to do something and that I am the one who knows what you should do.

[*Pause . . .*]

P: [*reflectively*] It is difficult—living with her—but I suppose I just have to understand her—I suppose I don't have to *do* anything—I can see that she could feel terrible and sort of very inadequate because she can't be different and she can't make sense of the work we do. I think she is the one who always thinks we have to do something and you have to tell me.

[*Pause . . . looking thoughtful . . .*]

Realizing they were her thoughts and not mine—the grim reaper thoughts—was the first time really that I have recognized her—outside of a session. Usually I'm all confused with her. I didn't think what you thought, that she feels I'm killing her, but I did realize it was her, and I tried very hard to remember what had happened so I could tell you today. . . . I hoped I would remember because I thought if I could, we would work out what happens to her. When I lose it all and forget [*speaking faster*], then, of course, I don't know how to understand anything [*speeding up even more*]—I can't understand her—that's why I wanted to remember.

T: She seemed to start speeding up as you began to voice your recognition of the value of holding onto your memories and your wish to tell me your experiences. . . . I wonder if this is because she again wants to rush through this exploration so that you and I can't work out what happens and so she can remain hidden. You seem very clear that once you have for-gotten the sequence of events and her thoughts you cannot understand her and why she is reacting the way she is. You think it is helpful to understand her, but she assumes you would only judge her as horrible. . . .

P: Or a nuisance because she can't change—I think she does feel very ugly and unwanted. She feels she can't do this therapy—she can't do it—she feels useless.

T: It does seem that the very understandings that you find helpful make her feel worse. You were keen to come today, but perhaps she delayed you because she didn't want to come to a session.

P: Yes, she didn't want to come. . . . As I differentiate myself from her, I feel better because I can be myself—I'm not all confused with her, but she feels this is horrible.

This was the end of the session.

Discussion

The noisy activity in the ladies' toilet before the session alerted me to the likelihood of the patient's cohabitee being present and mine responding.

It seems there is evidence, from before the beginning of the session to the end, that the patient wants to relate to me and use her mind. She tries hard to remember and understand the thoughts about the grim reaper, which she has identified as her internal cohabitant's thoughts and which she has recognized as being a response to her capacity to relate both to me and to Johnny her way, which is to engage in a two-way communication and to be able to separate without dread. She also shows an interest in understanding the reactions of her internal cohabitee in the ses-sion. However, at every stage she experiences considerable oppo-sition to achieving her aims.

Firstly, she has trouble actually getting into the consulting-room (she is held up in the toilet) and then she has trouble remembering the previous session. Then the cohabitee tries to rush through the session at a fast pace and uses lay psychiatric language of "highs and lows", which obscures an understanding of the cohabitee's state of mind. At key moments in the session the cohabitee again panics and tries to rush through the session and allow no opportunity for thinking more fully about her—for example, when the patient is being particularly lucid about the value for herself of differentiating herself from her cohabitee and having space to be herself. Another key moment is when Ms J realizes that her cohabitee has a concrete conviction ("symbolic equation", see Segal, 1957) that differentiation means separation, which for the cohabitee literally means cutting her heart (self) in half, and that would, of course, kill her.

When the patient realizes how essential it is for her survival to differentiate herself from her cohabitee and have her own space, the internal cohabitee feels that for her survival it is essential to prevent this. The opposition is the cohabitee's attempt to prevent herself from being murdered. She feels she is being murdered both by the patient differentiating herself from the cohabitee and by the patient relating to her boyfriend and to me. She feels completely excluded from the patient's relationships. Differentiation is dreaded because she is certain that when she is seen as separate and different from the patient, she will be discarded, because she is convinced that she can only be seen as horrible, ugly, a nuisance, and unable to engage in the therapy or to change. Given these convictions, she understandably opposes the therapy. We had further confirmation of the belief that differentiation was being experienced as the source of the murder by the cohabitee when Ms J arrived at the next session. In the session she reported that as she had walked up the stairs, she had caught sight of me on the landing, and the first thought was, "there is the executioner", accompanied by an image of a scaffold. When we explored this further, the patient concluded that her cohabitee sees not only me but also Ms J as her executioner. Before I understood the internal cohabitee's conviction that the aim of the therapy was to murder her, I used to think of the opposition as sabotage—that it was the patient who was sabotaging her own progress and that she had to recognize and own this.

The belief that differentiation is equivalent to murder occurs with patients other than those with manic–depressive diagnosis. This is because the characteristics of the psychotic personality have certain shared features, whatever the diagnosis. But with patients with bipolar illness the belief is intense, and this always needs to be recognized, otherwise the cohabitee will be misunderstood as a nuisance or a saboteur, which will confirm the cohabitee's worst fears.

The clinical material shows two of the particular difficulties with manic–depressive patients—or to be more accurate, "patients with manic–depressive cohabitees". These are the speeding-up process that begins to take the patient over at various points in the session and the pressure on the therapist to tell the patient what to do. Both these reactions can be difficult for the psychotherapist. I could have quoted from sessions where I have been taken over by my own cohabitee (and "forgotten" what I know) and become either very confused or irritated as the patient spoke faster and faster or just as manic as the cohabitee and trying to respond to everything the patient says. There have also been sessions where, when the patient had asked what to do, I have responded by doing exactly that—giving advice. This always confuses the patient as she loses me as her thinking partner.

In the session just described I was in touch with—but not pushed by—internal and external pressures to become manic, instruct the patient to slow down, or tell her what to do. I was helped to stay in an analytic mode by holding on to my knowledge of the patient's cohabitee and mine. In fact, the patient helped by referring to her knowledge that I too have an "ill one". Thus, nearly all my comments were directed towards helping the patient differentiate herself from her internal cohabitee and then work out why her cohabitee was so disturbed. This involved understanding the internal cohabitee's perceptions of herself, the therapist, and the patient and her relationships, which the cohabitee experiences as excluding her. Understanding the latter's perceptions enabled both of us to understand the terrifying world she inhabits and thus why she is in a manic state at this stage in the therapy. Ms J, in realizing she is not her cohabitee, was able to think about and understand this other person's point of view without being taken over by it. She was able to slow down and speak at her own pace.

She then expressed compassion for her cohabitee and realized that the latter's worst fears of differentiation leading to murder were misplaced and were due to that one's concrete thinking. Finally, Ms J realized that she did not have to do anything but instead would use her mind to understand her cohabitee.

Clinical addendum

Two years after this session the patient was able to begin discussing the end of her therapy, and an end date was set for 18 months ahead. This was a very difficult time because, even though the cohabitee perceived the therapy as murder, she was also equally convinced that the plan to end was in order to get rid of her as something horrible. Many sessions near the end were missed. However, the ending was achieved, and in that same year Ms J married Johnny. She contacted me some months after the ending to say that, although there were difficulties, she was enjoying married life. She indicated that she was able to hold her cohabitee in mind and recognize the cohabitee's fears and terrors, which inevitably still occur. She conveyed that she understood that it is a responsibility for the rest of her life to look after her internal cohabitee.

Concluding comments

In preparing this chapter, I realized more fully how the theory of internal cohabitation brings some of the strengths of both the Independent and Kleinian traditions into one framework, and how my own development as a psychoanalytic psychotherapist has been influenced by both traditions.

I think it is clear from the chapter how much I have drawn and gained from the work of the Kleinians and Post-Kleinians in the exploration and explication of the psychotic mind.

Much of the chapter builds on the work done in recognizing the characteristics of psychotic modes of thought and object-relating (or part-object–relating).

What I have gained from the work of Independents is probably less clear, and yet it is equally important. It is an attitude towards patients that is best summed up in Casement's title of his book, *On Learning from the Patient* (1985). Those who have read this book will know that listening to the patient involves hearing unpalatable things about oneself as a therapist, which may turn out, on examination, to be true rather than a distortion. The patient has the capacity to be a genuine partner in identifying and exploring transference phenomena and in recognizing countertransference enactments and can assist the therapist in his or her understanding of the patient and in how to make interpretations that the patient can use.

This is not to say that those working within the Kleinian tradition do not respect their patients' capacities for perceiving reality or that those working within the Independent tradition do not recognize psychotic processes. However, Rayner (1991) suggests that one of the major differences between the Kleinians and Independents is in their understanding of the sources of pathology: the former tend to conceptualize the sources as innate and the latter as arising from "real, faulty object relations". Disturbed reactions in therapy can be either a misperception or misunderstanding of the therapist for internal reasons or an accurate perception of an inappropriate, insensitive, or denigratory interpretation or comment by the therapist. Working out who is disturbed and why requires a careful and open-minded exploration by both patient and therapist. This is assisted by the concept of internal cohabitation because the interactions of the internal cohabitees of patient and therapist can be seen and acknowledged. In addition, the extent of the disturbance caused to the cohabitees by the fruitful dialogue and exploration of patient and therapist can be anticipated better. This allows the paranoid and concrete mode of functioning of internal cohabitees to be more fully elaborated and understood.

CHAPTER THREE

How far is transference interpretation essential to psychic change?

Anne Tyndale

> "It is perfectly true, as philosophers say, that life must be understood backwards, but they forget the other proposition, that it must be lived forwards."
>
> Søren Kierkegaard (Journal entry 1843)

Psychoanalytic thinking today encompasses two theories of psychic change. One focuses on developmental failure, the other on neurotic disturbance caused by conflicts at a higher level of development. The distinction between them is important because each demands a different therapeutic response, but they are not mutually exclusive. Both theories are concerned with psychic structures formed to try to reduce pain and anxiety, either arising from trauma at a stage when the baby is still undifferentiated from the mother or from struggles between instinctual wishes and internal and external demands. These structures are established during childhood and may be either altered or reinforced in adolescence.

"Psychic structures" is an inappropriately concrete term. It is a metaphor for the conscious and unconscious attitudes and functions of the ego arising from very early phantasies and experiences, which, along with innate character, form the personality. They include ways of experiencing the self and the outside world that are dependent on the kind of relationship the individual has with his internal objects; these are representations of significant people in an individual's early life. Defensive measures of a neurotic, psychotic, or psychosomatic nature may be adopted in the face of real or perceived, external or internal assault, and especially in the face of separation. These pathological forms of mental functioning, which impose past conflicts onto the present and compulsively repeat outdated solutions, leave no room for new experiences and true ego expansion.

Psychoanalytic psychotherapy is a process that creates an opportunity for changing some of these structures through experiencing, in the present relationship with the therapist, ways of behaving, thinking, and dreaming, the dynamics of which belong to the past. It is through reflection on these experiences that new ego-strength is acquired and split-off parts of the personality may be integrated. The primary agent that helps to create this space for thought and adaptation is the reliability of the psychotherapeutic frame. Within this safe setting and with the help of free association and dreams, patients regress, allowing unconscious feelings, expectations, and wishes to emerge in the transference and the therapist's countertransference. The opportunity is provided to make sense of the past and to disentangle it from the present.

The process by which distortions originating from experiences and unconscious phantasies relating to the past are projected onto elements in present-day life was called "transference" by Freud. He described it as a "false connection" (Freud, 1895d) between a figure from the past and one in the present onto whom earlier unconscious wishes—which he saw mostly as sexual—were transferred. The important point about this phenomenon was that the patient believed that the feelings experienced in this way were appropriate and was unaware of their past origins. At the time Freud saw transference as an obstacle to cure. By 1914, however, he was no longer viewing it in terms of random projections which caused trouble, but as a means of understanding a patient's inner world structured around infantile wishes, anxieties and conflicts which had never been satisfactorily managed (Freud, 1914g). Freud saw that the analytic situation, in which the real attributes of the therapist were for the most part undisclosed, encouraged an intensity of transference feelings, which might then be examined by the patient and therapist.

Sometimes, however, patients bring to sessions transference relating to people other than the therapist. Strachey (1934) considered interpretations of these "extra-transference" scenarios to be an important preliminary to interpretation of the transference towards the analyst, which, because of its immediacy, he deemed more truly mutative. As Harold Stewart (1973) has described, however, understanding of transference relating to someone other than the therapist can bring about important insight and significant change. Sometimes, too, a patient needs to keep the therapist apart from what he experiences as dangerous feelings in his inner world in order to maintain trust and a safe-enough environment to promote self-observation and mourning. To experience the therapist in the transference as a perpetrator of the terrors of his childhood can be felt to be overwhelmingly painful and frightening and may make it impossible for the patient to keep in sight the benign experience offered in reality.

Eventually, with the diminishing of persecutory guilt (Grinberg, 1978) and the expectations of a harsh superego, the patient may be able to enlarge his ego capacities and self-esteem sufficiently to explore hitherto "unthinkable anxieties" (Winnicott, 1962) in the transference, but, equally, this may never happen, and true integration will not be achieved. Even so, such a patient may still manage significantly to alter his psychic structures. Perhaps because of their limited outcomes it seems that the achievements in the therapies of these patients are not granted due respect. Transference interpretation is often seen as the hallmark of psychoanalytic psychotherapy, causing therapists trained in this way of working to feel that unless they are using it, they are incompetent or lazy. I shall now discuss these issues using my work with two different patients for illustration. I shall also consider timing and different kinds of transference interpretations.

Freud was exclusively concerned with the person of the analyst as a transference figure. Over the past fifty years, however, patients whose lives have been held up because of early environmental failure rather than neurotic conflict have more frequently sought psychoanalytic help, and it has been noted that transference phenomena do not only apply to the therapist himself but also to the whole psychoanalytic setting (Joseph, 1985). Many borderline patients are acutely sensitive to their surroundings and seek safety in a reliable frame. They sometimes feel so vulnerable that even the changes within this frame are experienced as unbearable, and for a while they may cling to an omnipotent—and, of course, illusory—belief that because sessions are regular and breaks and weekends predictable, they have control over them. These patients need the sureness of a safe place in which they can experience "continuity of being"—as Winnicott (1960d) describes it—as in the very early days of infancy, when the baby is unaware of the difference between himself and his environment, which he believes to be under his omnipotent command. Changes in times of sessions or the furniture in the room may be responded to as sudden attacks or threats of being dropped by a maternal presence, which under optimal circumstances should be taken for granted as reliable and which is symbolized in the psychotherapeutic frame.

Mrs L

The reaction of one of my patients, Mrs L, to the changed time of a session illustrates this point. It signified a serious disruption to her sense of "continuity of being"; in the transference she relived a sudden awareness of separateness between her mother and herself that had led her to adopt various kinds of pathological means of trying to protect her developing ego against the "unthinkable or archaic anxiety which results from failure of holding in the stage of absolute dependence" (Winnicott, 1962). However, understanding her fears about an unreliable environment was, at this stage, of much more use to her than any attempt to link the experience to her past.

She said she had been undisturbed by the change, but she spent nearly 50 minutes telling me that she always went to parties early because she was afraid of not finding her friends' houses and of failing to secure a place for herself when she arrived. She had to take control of her own safety because she could not rely on others to be dependable. When I interpreted a connection between her friends and her therapist who had changed a session, she was unable to recognize it. Mrs L thus let me know about her fears while preserving in her own mind the safety of the therapy. If she had allowed herself to experience me as the uncommitted mother of her past, she might never have returned. Her inner objects were so split that she did not have the capacity to hold two views of me in mind at the same time. In any case, to admit that her safety depended partly on another person would, for her, have constituted failure; she would have felt that she had let herself down by allowing another to have meaning in her narcissistic world of supposed self-sufficiency. My transference interpretation was therefore, at this time, unacceptable to her.

Michael Balint (1968) described in detail how, he felt, psychoanalytic methods could be helpful to patients who, like Mrs L, were suffering from environmental deficit, which prevented the development of a sense of self. He insisted that it was necessary to return to the trauma of this "basic fault" in order to make a "new beginning". Like Winnicott (1960d), he advocated no interpretations of the transference that drew attention to another person or relationship that the patient was not ready to encompass. He said that it was essential for the therapist to provide a safe space that depended on the unintrusive presence of a responsive and nonreactive therapist, as well as the regularity and predictability of the analytic setting. Keeping strictly to the analytic rules helps the patient gradually to appreciate his own boundaries and separate self, as well as those of the therapist.

Balint emphasized that it was essential for the analyst not to set himself up as a powerful or magical figure, because this would encourage a clinging or otherwise distancing relationship and would interfere with the patient's opportunity to find out more about himself and his own potential. Interpretations may be experienced as attacks, instructions, or someone else knowing best and therefore may help to perpetuate the establishment of a "false" (Winnicott, 1960b) or defensive self, which fits in with an environment felt to be intrusive and unempathic, inhibiting the discovery of true wishes and needs. They may also encourage projections of ego capacities such as thinking, which strip the patient of his own strengths.

A gate into my garden is usually open. One day, on leaving the house, Mrs L noticed that it was closed. She felt that this was a signal that she should not be there. She had also noticed a fleeting wish to go through it, which seemed to her tantamount to having done so. She told me that she felt it was wrong to be curious or interested, not so much about things as about people. This private garden was also associated in my patient's mind with growing plants, and I could have interpreted her curiosity as pertaining to my body and sexual consciousness; had I drawn attention to them, I would indeed have appeared as powerful and magical.

At this stage, to interpret to Mrs L that she wanted to intrude upon me would almost certainly have been experienced by her as a hostile attack, endorsing the sado-masochistic relationship that tended to govern her inner world. Another possibility would have been an alternative suggested by Steiner (1993), in which aspects of the patient projected onto the analyst are confronted in that location. For instance, I could have said that perhaps Mrs L thought I was wanting to shut her out of the garden. This shifts the focus from the patient to the therapist, making it easier for the patient to think. In this case, Mrs L's fears about being excluded and unwanted could then have been discussed. Such interpretations help the patient to feel understood: this is often a prerequisite to gaining understanding arising from patient-focused interpretations, addressing the patient's need to take responsibility for himself and for change. There is a danger, however, that an analyst-centred interpretation might be heard as a "countertransference confession" (Grinberg, 1978); Mrs L might have understood me to say that I did want to shut her out.

It seemed, at this point, most important to create space in which to explore her ways of thinking: her belief that everything that happened was in reference to herself, her inability to see a difference between thought and action, and her immobilizing inhibition about curiosity, which disallowed room for the exploration of thoughts and fantasies. The session focused on the discomfort the patient experienced from her perceptions of unpleasant sensations both arising from within her and imposed from outside, not on the way she related to me or the external world. It was part of a gradual process in which she could establish a sense of who she was, in a safe, unviolated space.

Winnicott's concept of holding has been very important in my work with Mrs L. He emphasized (1958) the importance of the infant being able to experience an "unintegrated" state in a completely safe environment, unintruded upon by any external impingement to which he needed to react: "In this setting the sensation or impulse will feel real and be a truly personal experience." Since being in therapy, Mrs L has been able to experience feelings that she could hitherto neither be aware of nor own because she had been occupied in warding off what she perceived to be dangerous and perpetual impingements from the outside world. Some of these have been painful feelings of attachment and others hostile ones.

It was a long time before Mrs L could bring herself to use the word "hate", which meant for her the loss of all connection or love—in other words, psychic death. Towards the end of the second year of her treatment, however, she began to describe to me fantasies of ruthlessly torturing her neighbour, whom she experienced as demeaning of her abilities and disregarding of her rights. She wanted me to ratify her unmitigated rage towards anyone who imposed his wishes upon her without asking her first. Behind her neighbour lay the internal images of her uncle and aunt who brought her up, and whom she perceived as never interested in her needs or point of view; muddled up with them also was her therapist, who ended sessions when she herself wished to stay. The transference was interpreted in the here-and-now, but a link with the past at this time might have been felt by the patient to be a way of lessening the impact of her fury and therefore an indication that I could not maintain the safe holding environment that demanded that I keep a firm sense of my own separateness. My job also was to bear in the countertransference, under the onslaught of the patient's fury, the feeling of my separate existence being ignored; this was also an experience of the patient's own past, which, in the reversal of roles, she re-enacted with me.

Freud (1914c) recognized countertransference as the "result of the patient's influence on (the physician's) unconscious feelings" and that "No psychoanalyst goes further than his own complexes or internal resistances permit". He thus saw countertransference as an impediment that needed to be removed by the therapist's own analysis and self-awareness. As a result of work initiated by Paula Heimann (1950), the concept is nowadays used much more widely and is recognized as a useful tool for understanding the internal world of the patient. At times a patient may wish to disown strong feelings that are projected onto the therapist, who then unconsciously identifies with them and acts upon them.

An example of this was when Mrs L had to cancel a session. She nonchalantly announced the fact, and before I knew where or who I was, I found myself offering her an alternative time. It was only afterwards that I understood that she had projected onto me her fear of losing our connection and, identifying with her panic, I had taken inappropriate action. I could then consider whether to interpret that she wished me to experience her fears in order to be rid of them herself, or whether she might have experienced such an interpretation to be a sign of my inability to endure her feelings, which she also found unbearable. In this case I would need to hold her projections until she was ready to own them. In this example it can be seen that countertransference is used by the patient as a creative means of communication.

Giovacchini (1979) points out that a transference interpretation may sometimes be made as a way of trying to manage the patient's feelings or behaviour. The effect of this is to step outside the therapeutic role, and it constitutes an imposition on the patient. The issue was made clear to me when a borderline patient was soon to take several weeks' break from therapy for reasons beyond his control. I said I thought that his state of mind during the separation would depend on how much he could hold on to the good connection he had developed with me. In response he said that he felt just as he did when his father insisted on him riding a horse he could not control. My comment, although correct, felt like a demand that he should manage feelings about which he was extremely uncertain; it probably arose from my unwillingness to bear knowing that he might well be plunged into dark emptiness during my absence and that neither of us would be able to do anything about it. It might have been more helpful to the patient if I had also acknowledged this possibility.

The psychoanalytic psychotherapist who has an understanding of what is being repeated in the transference cannot always lighten his burden by sharing it with the patient; such holding can be very hard work, and it is in these situations that consultation in supervision or with colleagues is often most valuable. Giovacchini reminds us that the observing ego of some of our most disturbed patients is not the outcome of flexibility but denotes a guarded attitude towards themselves and the outside world. It is only within the context of an unthreatening analytic situation, free from the therapist's own needs and desires, that this kind of vigilance can be dropped. He discusses the establishment of a "therapeutic alliance" (Zetzel, 1970), "treatment alliance" (Greenson, 1974) or "positive factor". However, anything coming from the therapist that is positively encouraging could be experienced as intrusive, and this unknown factor might be better described in terms of nothing negative—the "taken-for-granted background of safety" that Sandler (1960) describes, where there is no judgement or expectation.

Mr K

The second patient whom I will discuss is Mr K, who came to see me in a state of panic after being sacked—as he felt, unjustly—from a job he had thought to be secure. He felt so vulnerable and near to breaking down that he had to take control and create his own safe environment in a fused relationship with his therapist; he banished from consciousness any fear of unreliability or rejection. Breaks were barely acknowledged, and no reference was made to my existence outside the hours I spent with him. Some years later, however, Mr K was able to acknowledge the relationship with his therapist as "real", indicating that he knew it was not entirely within his control and that he had meaning for me as a separate person; he could then begin to mourn the death of his mother. I want now to consider six years of psychoanalytic psychotherapy during which, despite an increase in trust, the patient has adamantly set his own terms—namely, that interpretations of the negative transference are not to be acknowledged.

Interpretation of the transference is necessary as an agent for the integration of a child-self searching for absent objects created in phantasy and an adult-self making the best of what is available. Hopes need to be mourned in order for reality to be appreciated. The cost of achieving this kind of integration may, however, be more than some of our patients are prepared to pay, and Freud's (1912e) admonition that we should relinquish "therapeutic ambition" is important to bear in mind.

One of the purposes of assessment is to decide whether the patient's aims in seeking psychoanalytic psychotherapy have enough in common with those of the therapist to make the treatment sustainable. If pursuit of gratification or magical change seems to be the only aim in mind, it is unlikely that the patient will tolerate difficulties that arise in the therapy. The assessor must also consider whether the patient has enough ego-strength to bear frustration; this is sometimes difficult to know. This patient came in such a regressed and terrified state that I had to rely on his account of his relationships and achievements over his past life, to assess how strong his capacity for change might be. His presenting state also made it difficult to know what he was coming for. It might be thought that the limitations of his achievement indicate unsuitability for psychoanalytic psychotherapy, but this is not Mr K's view: "If I hadn't come here, I don't like to think where I would be", he has often said.

After a few months of therapy Mr K declared that his aims had changed. He was no longer with me in order to avoid a state of near-collapse by "trying to bury his feelings in concrete" or to seek advice; he now wanted to discover more about himself and to gain a "safer foundation on which to stand". He had already found out, through his encounter with a strictly boundaried therapeutic setting, that self-understanding was a route to feeling safer. As his panic diminished, Mr K had been able to tell me more about the terrors of his childhood. He was brought up as the only child of a single mother whose behaviour was, for the most part, irrational. The interpretation that enabled him to re-state his aim in therapy consisted of a link I made between the traumatic experience of being sacked from work and the feelings of a child at the mercy of an unreasonable mother who seemed to want to get rid of him. Mr K told me of the "enormous impact" of the liberating effect of gaining a historical perspective on his recent pain. "Now the re-learning begins", he declared. "The black mystery is solved."

He could start to learn more about himself and how to manage his feelings. This interpretation was not a transference one but was undoubtedly mutative in that it enabled the patient to find a new way of observing himself. For the first time in his life he was able to revisit the past in which he had struggled to survive in terrifying, lonely solitude, which, he felt, no one else could bear to enter. This return to the past was an agent for psychic change; the patient rediscovered good aspects of himself and faced ones he had felt too bad about to remember.

In her interviews with 65 analysts in America and Britain, Victoria Hamilton (1996) found that "Most contemporary psychoanalysts choose to focus their interpretations on the here-and-now analytic relationship" (p. 226). She wrote:

> Memory was often portrayed as something absent, where affect had paled with the passage of time. In contrast the present relationship was imbued with intensity of feeling. But this is not always the case. For, in addition to conveying information, memories of specific events in a person's life carry dramatic conviction; a memory sweeps the person up in an emotional storm. The memory has psychic force, imploding events in present time. [p. 228]

She adds that those analysts who did use reconstructive interpretations felt they were an important adjunct to the development of a sense of self and continuity of being.

Mr K has continued to make sense of himself; he has explored current relationships in the light of his past experiences and unconscious phantasies and has managed to separate out internal from external reality. For instance, now, in a different job, he encounters seniors who try to exploit him by expecting him to work long hours, but he no longer feels his existence is at stake if he refuses to fit in with them; he has a much firmer sense of his own needs and rights.

Alvin Frank (1991) quotes Freud's view of the analyst "in search of a picture of the patient's forgotten years, trustworthy and in essential respects complete", but he insists that the psychoanalytic experience must go deeper than this. The experience in the transference must subjectively approximate the inner meaning of the patient's childhood events in order that these can fully be understood as the foundation for the patient's psychological strategies and structures. This provides the opportunity for the rewriting of the patient's autobiography, which is essential for true psychic change. There is now the opportunity for a more realistic examination of options available in present-day life, which were not possible when pathological solutions were found. The essential difference between the rewriting of autobiography as achieved by Mr K and that described by Alvin Frank lies in Mr K's unwillingness to acknowledge the way in which he relives the past in the transference; he thus denies himself an opportunity for experiential memory by relegating current feeling to an appropriate time in childhood.

There have on a few occasions been manifestations of feelings in the transference, experienced psychosomatically rather than psychically, which have led the patient to comment that the symptoms might be a way of remembering being physically abused by his mother. One such occurrence was before an Easter break, when Mr K came to a session with swollen tonsils. He had woken that morning with a horrible feeling of being stifled, and he wondered whether he was re-living an experience of his mother having tried to stuff something down his throat; he said it made him feel disloyal even to consider it. In association he told me how choked he had felt when he was sacked. In his mind he was linking the mental pain of feeling abandoned by his abusive mother and the physical trauma. He said he was not concerned about the break because he knew I would be there when he returned. When I said that perhaps there was another self who was not so sure, the patient told me he could not "get the hang" of what I said.

In this session Mr K could only risk bringing the past into the present by maintaining a split. He described to me the horrors of the past while experiencing them somatically, but the emotional feeling was left for me to undergo through chilling feelings in the countertransference. "Disloyalty" to his mother would mean acknowledging the persistent trauma of her emotional absence from him and risking the annihilating catastrophe of their mutual rage. Unlike Mrs L, therefore, he could not get in touch with his ruthless fury without being afraid that both he and his object would perish. Although in leaving him for two weeks I was evidently associated with the abandoning mother, Mr K was making clear his terror that a re-living of the past might overwhelm the present and cause pain he could not bear.

Victoria Hamilton (1996) quotes from Kierkegaard's journal of 1843: "It is perfectly true, as philosophers say, that life must be understood backwards, but they forget the other proposition, that it must be lived forwards". This seems particularly appropriate for this patient, who is understanding his life backwards but also living forwards because he has decided not to break down in the middle. In the same way that psychosomatic symptoms unconsciously communicate proof of psychic survival (McDougall, 1989), so did Mr K secretly tell me of his inner life through dreams, but he would not allow my interpretations to make their meaning conscious. "I can see why you say that", he might tell me, "but it doesn't mean anything". Both Cecily de Monchaux (1978) and Harold Stewart (1973) have described the use of dreams as depositories for aspects of the self that the ego cannot yet manage. A function of the dream may be to evacuate or store intolerable states of mind but they are also told as a means of communication. Klauber writes, "What is added to the general conditions governing the report of a dream in the conditions of psycho-analysis is an achievement by the ego of a new relationship to the libidinal object, since, as has been indicated, for the first time the dreamer has acquired the possibility of being understood" (Klauber, 1967).

Mr K has wanted to be understood, but his wish for understanding (Steiner, 1993) has been limited. When he told me a dream about meeting his former partner who ignored him, he communicated his fear, but he did not want the relationship with me drawn into it. A terrified self could not bear to contemplate that I might ignore him and was unwilling to use the transference for play in which different realities could be tossed about to find some way of co-existing. The transitional space that the transference might have provided, has, however, been found in dreams. Through dreaming, Mr K has given me much information about his psychic life in the expectation that I will respect it and keep it in mind. At other times he has also used dreams for psychic work in the way that Masud Khan (1972) described when an integrative experience, no longer acted out, is acknowledged through dream-ing. One such dream showed a disappointed but accepting aban-donment of the hope of finding a homosexual partner who would, by representing his ego ideal, transform him. This hope is no longer acted out in a promiscuous search for partners—Mr K now lives in an ordinary, companionable relationship. This important change, which has required genuine mourning and conscious sac-rifice of excitement, has been made possible by strict adherence to therapeutic boundaries.

These boundaries may be understood to represent a "third" presence in psychoanalytic psychotherapy. Throughout therapy there is a transference towards the "other parent" who makes it impossible for wishes of fusion or sole possession to be fulfilled and who eventually helps to set the child free from parental ties. Christopher Bollas (1996) sees dream interpretation in terms of the child-self having the dense experience of the dream that, in the waking reverie of free association with the therapist, is shared as if in the holding relationship with the mother. Interpretations that bring the inner and outer worlds together are, however, the do-main of the thinking father, without whom these important ways of knowing can never be complete. As the interpretations become absorbed, so mother and child, with the help of father, become more differentiated. In bringing to me the dreams that he hopes I will understand, Mr K may have found a father whom his jealous, possessive mother would never allow him to know, but sadly this father must be kept secret.

The therapeutic boundaries have gradually been experienced by Mr K as liberating and have enabled him to stop having to assert his independence by missing sessions. Gaps between ses-sions and especially at weekends, longer breaks, awareness of other patients, and the limits to the relationship with the therapist such as paying fees and ending sessions on time are constant re-minders of adult life, in which therapist and patient live equally and separately and which, little by little, the patient accepts as reality. "A good-enough mother", writes Gregorio Kohon (1986b, pp. 59–60), "is also someone who becomes more and more absent; she is not the one who loves us alone but one who has someone else to love and be loved by . . . her narcissism depends progressively less on the child." Our hope is to help our patients to gain autonomy.

I have often felt that I do not exist for this patient, and yet I have also known that my predictable presence, commitment, and the understanding I have offered have been vital. His split-off self has made me his own creation in order to make sure that he will never be at the mercy of an uncontrollable and uncontrolled object again, but at the same time he works with me in a relationship he feels is real. Fusion, says Badaracco (1992), is necessary in order to explore other ways of being and particularly to give up some identifications that have been adhered to when the environment has not been safe enough to allow a strong ego to develop; abandoning old identifications can be experienced as dangerous and painful. This patient has used the therapeutic space to build up ego-strength by discovering a view of himself as someone worth while; he has been able to give up his old idea of only being acceptable or wanted if he is putting things right for others. He can now use insight to separate figures in the present from those in the past. He is sure that he will never again experience the terror of feeling resourceless and alone in which he entered therapy. "These changes will stay", said Mr K recently, and I believe him. He knows that the therapy will end and is beginning to consider what the ending will signify.

In "On Beginning the Treatment" (1913c), Freud referred to "transference cure", which, he said, could not last. In her latest book, however, Nina Coltart (1996) gives a different view and cites three cases of "transference cure" that, she felt, brought lasting changes. Such a cure is dependent on an idealized transference in which disappointment and loss of hopes have not been worked through—a fantasied finding of a fantasied object. There is an element of this in the notion of internalizing a good object or identifying with a good analyst—the idea of having an inside figure who will not let us down. Many people find such an illusion, in various forms, a very helpful aid to getting through life, but it is vulnerable to disillusionment and detracts from the achievement of bearing responsibility for oneself. "We do not in fact 'offer' (our patients) anything 'good' or 'bad'", writes Gregorio Kohon , "what we offer them is very little. . . . Hopefully, what they get

from us is what I would call our *progressive absence*. . . . The success
of the analysis is not achieved through the identification with, or
incorporation of, the person of the analyst into the patient's inner
world. . . . The analysand will have to reconcile himself with the
fact that the primary object will never be found again" (1986b, pp.
59–60).

The patient can only do this, however, if he can continue to use
therapeutic space for reflection, and it is this capacity, it is to be
hoped, that our patients take away with them. Mr K has been able
to be in touch with the absence of his primary objects in a limited
way. He has brought together two versions of them—one idealized and the other denigrated—with a much more sympathetic
attitude, and he has been in touch with real sadness and disappointment about the deprivations of his childhood.

Some of these deprivations have been possible to bear because
Mr K has been able to appreciate the assets in his personality that
helped him to survive them. When he first came to therapy, he
was afraid that he would have to give up the person he knew
himself to be. He was very relieved when I interpreted a dream
about *using old floorboards to build a new kitchen* in terms of making
use of the "floor" of his own strengths to gain a more creative and
nourishing way of seeing himself and his life. Paula Heimann's
(1957–59) ideas are very important in helping us to understand a
patient such as this. She sees the ego according to Freud's later
view of it: not just as a product of the id or the result of identifications, but as containing genetic qualities of its own, independent
of emotional experience. She expressed a firm belief in the capacities of patients and the importance of enabling them to be free
enough to use them. Life does not just consist of an inner world:
real experiences must not be discounted, nor should hereditary
attributes. It is important that the cruel circumstances of Mr K's
upbringing and their lasting toll should be acknowledged, but
equally his ego-strengths, which have helped him to get through
life, must be respected. He has looked after himself through childhood and through his therapy, setting his terms when he feels
survival is at stake and knowing what he feels is right for him.

Heimann (1949/50) talks of patients who use their environment to make up for deprivations: other identifications are gath-
ered in order to compensate for the poverty of the original objects.

This ability presupposes, however, a "healthy narcissism without which an individual cannot put his abilities to good use"; Mr K's "healthy narcissism" has expanded over his years of therapy, and he is still gathering in compensatory experiences—a process that began in early childhood.

This therapy has been truly psychoanalytic, according to Freud's (1912e) definition. He stated that the doctor should be opaque to his patients like a mirror and show them nothing but what is shown to him. In her 1968 paper Enid Balint describes two phases of the mirroring technique. In the first phase, the analyst identifies with the patient, and secondly, shows him what his ideas and thoughts look like to her. Later in the paper she talks of the loneliness that friendliness can engender in a patient. If I had been drawn into Mr K's wish for "friendliness", the healthier aspects of his personality would have responded with gratification, but this would have spelt death to a primitive self desperate to be recognized. In the neutrality of the therapeutic setting, a new sense of himself—with wishes, needs, and a right to choose—has emerged. "I remember the day", he said to me recently, "when on leaving a session I wanted to dance in the street, shouting, 'I have rights. I have rights!'" He no longer felt he had to put himself aside in order to stave off attacks from a mad maternal figure, and some of his instinctual self and creativity could come into being with a new perception of object relationships. He is able to claim the bringing about of this psychic change as his own achievement; he feels proud of himself and wants me to be proud of him, too.

The achievement has, however, been partial. Enid Balint (1968) points out that mirrors reflect indiscriminately, and she talks of the analyst using the mirroring technique with discretion. The person reflected also has some say in the matter, however, in that he can turn the mirror around or move away. The way Mr K did this whenever the negative transference was reflected and his possible reasons for doing so were thoroughly explored; had I tried to insist on this type of reflection, he would probably have left, possibly in a painful psychotic transference that would have denied him the chance to make use of the therapeutic space in the way that he has.

Mourning involves not only the acceptance of reality, as Freud states, but also being able to see the object and self as separate wholes. The destructive splits between pathological selves and objects lessen, allowing a whole self and whole object, imperfect but good-enough, to be found. This bringing-together of idealized and denigrated objects is part of an infant's developmental process. It takes place during the gradual differentiation of inner and outer reality, past and present, which happens in the transitional space between mother and child, or therapist and patient, described by Winnicott (1951). This is creative space; it provides a third dimension to life in which two worlds can meet, with all their opposites and contradictions. Within it a child can play, unrestricted by the demands of reality or of an inhibiting inner world.

Mr K has been on his guard since birth. He has known nothing of the experience of playing safely: in childhood, wherever he was, he always expected a rageful mother suddenly to appear and attack him. The watchfulness was directed not only towards an external danger, however, but also towards his internal hurt and rage, which—seeming equally dangerous—he could not allow himself to feel. The need for self-supervision has often made him feel as if he is in a prison from which he will never escape; but to abandon it in order to allow regression in the therapy would have felt like jeopardizing his existence. He has, however, while experiencing safety in a positive relationship with me, allowed himself to feel furious rage towards a boss whom he sees as trying to exploit him; perhaps, too, telling me dreams has been a way of alleviating some of the burdens placed upon his sentinel-self.

The splits in his psyche remain, and only the accessible conscious and pre-conscious feelings can be brought into the play space of the psychotherapy. Here free association, which at first was inhibited by fears of my derision, can now be enjoyed, and some valuable working-through has been achieved by gradually allowing awareness of past experience to emerge. A "safer foundation" has, therefore, been created, but there is always the cellar shut off beneath it. Freud (1920g) stressed that in order to make use of transference interpretation, the patient must be able "to recognize that what appears to be reality is, in fact, only a reflection of a forgotten past": the dire consequences of finding that he does not have this ability are ones that my patient is not prepared to risk. If the playful quality in the transference, which recognizes its "as if" nature, gets lost, hope for change disappears, and new experience cannot be appreciated.

During my six years of work with this patient I have, at intervals, felt frustrated. This has sometimes resulted from a countertransference communication when Mr K has wanted me to experience how his creativity and initiative had constantly been curtailed by his mother. Sometimes, however, it has been because my own wishes for the therapy have been different from those of the patient, and I have felt disheartened by the limitations of the work. It has not been easy to accept the restrictions that Mr K will always have to bear and to have faith in his use of the therapeutic space to bring about lasting change—albeit keeping a split-off self that he fears to be mad but with which he feels he can now live more safely.

CHAPTER FOUR

The absent mother: splitting as a narcissistic attempt to find a solution

Judy Cooper

W hat has changed in psychoanalysis and psychoanalytic psychotherapy over the past two or three decades is the range of patients coming for help. The difficulties that people seeking treatment bring into therapy are increasingly the sort that Freud had felt could not benefit from psychoanalysis. Today, narcissistic and borderline patients present a challenge to the clinician, and the more recent theoretical insights help in the better understanding of severe disturbance. The opening up of pre-oedipal development—particularly the rigorous observation of the earliest stages of infant life by psychoanalysts such as Klein and Winnicott and their heirs—has altered the face of psychoanalytic treatment today.

In this chapter, by describing the work in a long-term, intensive psychotherapeutic treatment, I try to show how the absence of a safe, predictable, physically and emotionally present mother is one of the factors that underlies and encourages splitting in an attempt to avoid feelings of emptiness and the inability to connect with others. After some preliminary observations about the absent mother, splitting, and narcissism, I give a case illustration that demonstrates both the real possibilities and the limitations of what can be achieved with narcissistic patients.

The absent mother

Clinically, one sees despair and futility in the patient for whom separateness is intolerable and who is locked into a self-destructive pattern of behaviour and is desperately searching for the lost primary object. Whilst Kleinians emphasize the oral aspect of attachment, I believe that what the patient is seeking is the closeness and security of the womb (Cooper & Maxwell, 1995). This is particularly true where there has been a rupture in the person's experience of mothering, whether this is through the mother's physical or emotional absence. The immense difficulty in the work with this type of patient is their constant movement between merging and violently breaking off.

The mother is pivotal in emotional development (e.g. Winnicott, 1957, 1960c, 1960d). She is, for the baby, the first environment, biologically and psychologically. How the mother behaves and feels in relation to her infant will influence his health for the rest of his life. An absent, incapable, inconsistent, or tantalizing mother will lead to a lack of adequate mirroring, which frequently results in an idealized phantasy of merged mothering, with no separation. Keeping good and bad feelings safely apart is one of the main ways of preserving the idealized mother.

Money-Kyrle (1971) points out that the three basic facts of life that we all have to accept are the difficult realities of (1) recognizing the breast as a supremely good object, which means being able to accept one's helplessness and the possibility of dependency on a good external source for one's survival; (2) recognizing the parents' intercourse as a supremely creative act, which means being able to accept the primal scene and the Oedipus complex; and (3) recognizing the inevitability of time and ultimately death, which means facing the fact that everything ends, including access to the breast, and that the reality of death leads to a need for renewal. Adjusting to these "primal facts" is a monumental task for all of us. It involves acknowledging separateness and, consequently, loss. However, for the motherless patient who has resorted to narcissistic solutions, who oscillates between omnipotence and powerlessness, and who cannot readily identify with anything or register anything much outside himself, these tasks become impossible goals.

When a therapist is faced with continual attacks that threaten to rupture the therapeutic exchange and space, it is important to know patients for what they are. The therapist needs to remember that what the patient is really seeking is a safe and warm early experience. It is this frustrated search that fuels patients' inability to contain anything, their rigidity, their grandiosity and insistent need to control, their lack of symbolization, their tyrannical super-egos (a "gang" or "Mafia"), which leaves them no room for manoeuvre or to take anything in, and their refusal to acknowledge any positive experience or progress. Often where the mother has been absent or seriously disappointing, there is such a powerful idealization of her that it is almost impossible to get anywhere near the phantasy to try gradually to de-idealize mother and the fused relationship with her. Splitting is one of the main ways of maintaining this idealization. One such patient maintained a sharp divide between his inflated idea of his link with his impoverished mother and the paucity of what he received in his therapy. He was so barricaded against becoming ordinary and needing someone that he completely split off his vulnerable, needy self, being defensive, enraged, and destructive throughout his therapy with me. He could only tolerate a solution coming from *himself* and could not let anything in from me.

Splitting

Hanna Segal, in her dialogue with Jonathan Miller on "Kleinian Analysis", explains how splitting is an intrinsic part of the earliest developmental process:

> To me the death instinct is not a biological drive to return to the inorganic (as Freud described it) but it is a psychological

wish to annihilate this sudden change brought about by birth. So the infant is born into a sort of chaos of contradictory perceptions—pleasant and unpleasant—and of contradictory desires; very soon he starts to sort them out and the sorting out is called "splitting".... One is assailed by bad things, or one experiences something very ideal. [Segal, in Miller, 1983, p. 255]

Certainly, a degree of normal splitting is necessary for growth. Klein stressed, for example, that the distinction between mother and father can represent a perfectly acceptable form of splitting. However, we shall see how splitting can be pathological and involve a defensive misrepresentation that distorts reality and keeps a division going as part of an illusory integration.

Steiner (1993), in his excellent book, *Psychic Retreats*, views narcissistic resistances as part of a highly organized system of defence trying to deal with pathological fragmentation. In a seemingly paradoxical way, the narcissist uses splitting in an attempt to control overwhelming fragmentation. Steiner points out that there are two defensive ways of dealing with the discomfort afforded by reality: (1) "turning a blind eye" as exemplified by the myth of Oedipus; or (2) retreating to omnipotence. Both of these are primitive ways of responding for a patient who is in the area of paranoid–schizoid anxieties.

Narcissism

Narcissism essentially involves fragmentation and is not a coherent or cohesive state of mind. One of the most telling symptoms of narcissism is the difficulty the person encounters with sustaining any intimate relationship with another person. As Freud (1914c) says, every human being originally has two sexual objects—himself and the woman who nurses him. To what extent someone shows a preference for self-love as opposed to object-love in intimate relationships depends on that person's particular make-up and experiences.

The instinctual aim of narcissism—as of all pregenital aims—is to be loved, and narcissistic love involves a disturbance in development resulting in libidinal energy being focused on the self rather than on others. Thus, what Narcissus saw mirrored in the water when he looked at his reflection was the perfect lover he was longing for—the only problem was that it was not another person but himself, someone not separate but disconnected and unreal. This simple fact says it all, for the difficulties in grasping reality and the avoidance of self-knowledge, because it would involve the destruction of the perfect image, constitute the main active process of splitting in the narcissistic person (Cooper & Maxwell, 1995).

It is accepted across the different schools of psychoanalytic theory that narcissistic difficulties involve a disturbance in the experience of the self. Whether it is conscious or unconscious, the inability to register a separate other always involves a marked degree of grandiosity and an immense difficulty in acknowledging dependency. Narcissism is essentially a problem of separation, and, to some degree, we are all narcissistic. To an extent this is normal and healthy, as we all come from the helpless grandiosity of infancy: as Freud (1914c) said: "His majesty, the baby." This is known as "primary narcissism", the "objectless" stage in infancy when there is no awareness of any differentiation between self and other.

Due to the fact that narcissism covers a wide range of disturbance, it is important to discriminate between different degrees of severity. A person labelled "mildly narcissistic" is able to relate to others without seeing them exclusively as an extension of himself; this is impossible for someone who is "severely narcissistic", who would be more likely to hook his own projections and phantasies onto others. These differences will obviously influence the outcome of the treatment. Although the surface manifestations may vary and a person may display hysterical, obsessional, or phobic symptoms or even present what looks like a manic phase of a cyclical illness, the tell-tale feature is that the narcissist's core is split and feels dead.

Clinical illustration

Mʀ P

Mr P was in three-times-a-week psychoanalytic psychotherapy with me for eight years. Over this period his life changed considerably. When he came into therapy, he was 27 years old. Although he had a degree in mathematics, he was working as a clerk in a job he despised, and he wanted to find a more creative outlet for his energies. During his time in therapy he completed a foundation course in art, obtained a first-class degree in the subject, and finished his M.A. at a prestigious art college. By the time he left therapy, he had organized and was involved in several enterprising art projects and was planning to combine all this with some part-time administrative office work. He was very different from the depressed, passive, aimless young man, wearing mismatching socks, who found his way to my consulting-room half-an-hour late all those years ago. The socks and the lateness could be seen as his way of demonstrating mixed feelings about himself and therapy.

Mr P has recently ended his therapy with me. In the two main areas of life—work and relationships—he has undoubtedly made some progress. He has undeniably achieved much in relation to work, but as far as his relationships are concerned the improvement is more uncertain. The reason for this may be that he still uses splitting destructively and his psychic structures for integration are not yet firmly in place.

He has managed, through his artwork, to harness his grandiosity creatively, enhancing what is most genuine in himself and acquiring some ability to accept pleasure (Kohut, 1984). For a long time he would tend to over-rate his own productivity and creativity, whilst I would experience a real sense of sterility about his "fine thoughts"; this, however, was far less the case later on in his therapy. In the sphere of relationships I may have to accept that despite therapy he will never attain the objective of relating fully to another person but will oscillate between object-relating and narcissistic relating. Kohut (1984) called this "mature selfobject relations". As Mr P said teasingly to me when I pointed out the way he used splitting in his everyday relationships: "You should be pleased, after all these years of fantasy, at least I'm in a relationship", and it was certainly beneficial for him to be involved with someone externally, despite the continuous frustrations of the relationship. Apart from the masochism, the splitting in the situation (his own, his girlfriend's, and her other boyfriend's) fuelled his fear of eventually going mad like his sister and perpetuated his lifelong problem with integration.

Mr P, the eldest of four children from a wealthy upper-middle-class English family, has two brothers six and eight years his junior and a sister two years younger than he. His sister used to be his constant companion in play, but later she turned her attention to her two younger brothers. She is now married and has suffered from a severe psychiatric illness, having been treated in the past with ECT and subsequently with lithium. In this connection it is worth noting that Mr P's narcissism has often prevented him from acknowledging his need of me or of anyone else. It would seem that behind his denial is the terror that, if he admitted any vulnerability, he would turn out to be psychotic or, like his sister, would be faced with dealing with the basic struggles of life and survival. This ill, vulnerable sister is, I am sure, another factor colouring his relationships with women.

During therapy Mr P tended to belittle his sister's life, helping in a psychiatric community at quite some distance from her parents and family, but on further exploration we could see that there was some envy of her and the safe life she had managed to carve out for herself and her husband. In the transference this was something he would periodically attack about me. Both Mr P's younger brothers seem to have had a far less conflictual journey through life than either of their elder siblings. They have done conventionally well, going to the same schools and university as Mr P and attaining professional qualifications, and they also have active social lives.

Mr P regards his father, a merchant banker, as a workaholic quite removed from taking care of his children and unable to fulfil any nurturing functions, and his mother as supporting his father in everything he did. At his first session Mr P stated that not only did he have no memory of events before the age of 20, but he had had "no feelings about mother 'til a year ago". He went on to say that he felt very sad about not having any "history of relation-ships" and the fact that he had relied on himself for so long. He added that he had spent many hours rocking as a child.

In his therapy, whenever Mr P mentioned his mother, it was without much emotion. One had the sense of a strong parental couple, but of a mother who was remote and fairly inaccessible to her children, preoccupied with her own varied interests. She was never described as a present, holding mother but rather as absent. In the transference, although his fantasies focused on a longing for closeness, Mr P kept me distant, retreating into his world of ideas or, at times, missing a session to break the link with me if he felt that he had been understood too well or that we had touched on something particularly meaningful.

The family had had a nanny, and Mr P went to a preparatory boarding-school at 7 and at 13 to the same public boarding-school that his father and grandfather had attended. At school he was competent at his studies and an excellent athlete, but he was never one of the lads and often spent time alone, putting "Keep out" on his study door. In the transference I was soon made aware that he might put up a "Keep out" sign at any point by cutting himself off from me and escaping into his world of ideas or by missing a session. Mr P had a constant dilemma about coming to therapy, and because he was frightened of any change he was reluctant to let me and my thoughts into his internal world.

His mother had told him that his father fell in love with her because she was so "enigmatic", and certainly this has been a repeated theme in Mr P's therapy. The women who have excited him have represented the tantalizing and exciting maternal imago. They have not been constant, tender, or containing, and what has excited him is their capacity to tantalize and frustrate. There is undoubtedly a perverse, masochistic element to this, which is clearly illustrated in Mr P's current relationship with his girlfriend. In fact, Mr P was particularly critical of me when I was understanding. This may have been a painful reminder of his own mother's remoteness.

Although Mr P struggled with all manner of relationships over the years, including those with authority figures (father) and peers (siblings), in this chapter I concentrate on his interaction with women. At university he had been single-mindedly pursued by a fellow student, which satisfied his need that women should recognize *him*, and although there was an interval in their relationship whilst he went on holiday with someone else, they got back together again into an extremely merged asexual relationship. This had just broken up when Mr P came into therapy, and he was distraught about it. In fact, he remained the chief emotional partner on the sidelines throughout this woman's marriage to someone else (she rang him 20 minutes after her wedding ceremony), throughout her divorce, and throughout her subsequent involvements with other men. She has asked him on several occasions more recently whether they could set up home together and have children, but he has refused, recognizing both his own fear of intimacy and what he saw as her destructiveness in sexual relationships.

Soon after he started therapy, Mr P embarked on a relationship with one of his office colleagues. To begin with he was mesmerized by her and wanted to keep phoning her and be close to her. Then he found that he was impotent with her, but as soon as she became interested in him he lost his interest in her, whereupon he became potent. They went to India together. He resorted to a typically narcissistic way of relating whereby he could just bear to be with her if she did exactly what he wanted. If she did not, he became sadistic and rivalrous. This was recorded in his diary, which she came across and read. Not surprisingly, the affair soon ended, and for some years after this Mr P explored no real relationships.

He admired the girlfriends of his flatmates; one was very warm, another was training to be a therapist. As I pointed out, they seemed to be different versions of me. He constantly fantasized about all the young women around him on his art course. His co-students were all about 10 years younger than he was and reminded him of his university days. He was completely passive about these women, and often they were already spoken for or in some other way not available to him. There was a distinct split between his imagination and reality. He did not seem able to explore any possibility of finding a close relationship with another person. During this period he would pursue his wish to merge with an idealized object by taking warm baths that lasted for hours.

In the therapy we were engaged in a continuous struggle as to how to translate his omnipotence with the wonderful "ideas" floating around in his head into ordinary words so that he could communicate with another person. "Being ordinary" was anathema to Mr P, and he contemptuously attacked what was ordinary in me, his parents, and himself. At one stage he took up pottery and made some beautifully shaped pots, which he soon realized was an attempt to re-create a perfect primary object. Significantly, he gave two of them to his mother.

A recurrent theme right from the beginning of his therapy was Mr P's despair about how he was ever going to reach the source of his problems, as he could remember nothing much of his childhood, nor recall any dreams. This is an example of how he shredded and fragmented his experiences. Once, after a weekend break, when he had written me a letter to try to maintain the link with me, he described an incredibly beautiful landscape he had seen, with a mountain in it, representing a hug to him. He accepted the interpretation that it was much safer to derive gratification from scenery that he could control rather than expect the same reaction from me, who could withhold the hugs and desert him at weekends. In breaks it became a real problem for Mr P to find a way he could hold on to the relationship between us in my absence. Gradually he realized that I was important to him, and he managed to be in touch with his helplessness and say, just before a holiday break, "You dare leave me now". This may have been similar to his feelings of loss and abandonment on his separation from his mother when she disappeared to have more babies and when he was sent away to boarding-school.

Curiously, Mr P could feel an intense love of places from his past and an attachment to them. He sometimes recalled buildings and scenery in the minutest detail, "even the way the blades of grass lay" on his prep-school lawn, but his feelings about people or separations—for example, when he was sent away to boarding-school at 7—were entirely blank. Indeed, his obsessive observations had kept him going and had probably kept him sane, but he persistently forgot his feelings, and this was precisely what he had come into therapy for: to be in touch with his feelings—but to what extent dare he let that happen? As I previously mentioned, the problem with a patient like Mr P is the constant oscillation in the therapy between the wish to merge and the wish to attack and break contact. Indeed, he was frequently in a panic about the contemptuous, denigratory, enraged side of himself and would attack me and the therapy or shut down on any interaction between us. Nevertheless, he came regularly to his sessions, since part of him was helped and he knew this, and he was longing to find the more creative and reparative part of himself.

In his therapy I replaced his mother as the primary object who remained out of his control. He was angry with his parents and hated his upper-class background, the people, money, class, education, accent, even the gestures. He envied his flatmate, Rick, who could feel comfortable in the East End. At this time, when he was well into his therapy, he managed to remember a dream:

> There was a lost child on a high plateau. He could not work out who the child was. He [Mr P] was crippled and crawled up and down quite a few times to visit the child through rich silk surfaces. There were lots of people below who seemed to be related to Rick and to him. Rick wanted Mr P to reach the child, who seemed to be some relation of Rick's.

Mr P's strong association to the dream was of Quasimodo in the tower of Notre Dame. [This was in June 1991, well before the recent Disney version of The Hunchback of Notre Dame.]

Here we can see Mr P as the lost child with his dilemma of how to reach mother, for the Hunchback of Notre Dame was in love with a beautiful, inaccessible woman, Esmeralda. However, although the lost child was coming up in these images, he was not evident in Mr P's memories or feelings. Once again there was a split between the external image and the feelings buried inside. Was this the defence against the passionate little boy who idealized his parents and was betrayed by mother having more babies and sending him away to school? Perhaps Mr P wished to identify with Rick, who felt comfortable where he had grown up and whose working-class parents had not sent him away.

Sometimes in his most recent relationship there seemed to be progress, but often I saw it as a repetition of his unhappiness at, once again, being unable to find a mother who could relate to, focus on, and recognize him. Britt was a Swedish student at art college with Mr P. She was 26 and, like him, doing her M.A. She had a boyfriend, Stefan, in Sweden, whom she refused to give up and to whom she had a very strong attachment. The relationship between Britt and Mr P continued intermittently for almost two years, being interrupted by Stefan's and Brit's comings and goings to and from Sweden. When the Swedish couple were together, Mr P was usually ignored, with not so much as a telephone call. Britt periodically made it clear that if she *had* to choose between the two of them, she would choose Stefan, and he was the one with whom she saw herself sharing her life. To maintain a relationship with these conditions indicated a marked degree of masochism in Mr P. It seemed that it was this hurtful, rejecting attitude that both paralysed and, at the same time, stimulated and excited Mr P. Often I found myself feeling irritated and angry with the way he was being treated, and his friends would too, but he insisted he felt no anger at all. This is an example of projective identification, as he certainly succeeded in putting his angry feelings into me.

It was very difficult for Mr P to experience any conscious anger with Britt. Instead, he expressed it in his symptoms of cutting off emotionally and in his impotence with her and in his acting out by missing sessions with me. At times he was able to express his dissatisfaction with me, complaining that I was cold and "stuck" in my views whilst Britt was warm and flexible so that with her he felt free to be himself. By splitting the warmth and anger between Britt and myself, he managed to maintain a precarious picture of an idealized object.

Particularly in the closing six months before he left therapy, Mr P enacted his feelings by missing most of his sessions. Sometimes he let me know, sometimes not. I interpreted his offhand treatment of me and his sessions as acting out in his relationship with me what we had been unable to make him conscious of feeling. As we had not, as yet, been able to find the right words to reach him, he needed to show me how much Brit's behaviour was affecting him and just how pushed around and abused he felt. Following this interpretation, he was able to acknowledge his anger with Britt in brief bursts, although not in any sustained way. However, he was able to express his unease about the contemptuous way he was treating me and his therapy.

What marked the last phase of our work together was my refusal to be drawn into a sado-masochistic way of relating, being
treated in this dismissive way. We discussed the importance of
him valuing himself and his therapy enough for him to come
regularly and work at the outstanding issues in his life, or else to
decide to end the therapy. After some weeks of thought he said
that he would like to continue at least until the summer, but beyond that he might need to travel to pursue his artistic career and
his plans were too uncertain for him to make any concerted commitment to therapy. Nonetheless, although his conscious choice
was to continue with his therapy, he still continued to miss many
more sessions than he was attending. I put this to him and also
the fact that our association had gone on for a long time, and the
attachment was too important for us to allow it to disintegrate
in this way. I stressed that it was essential for him to put aside
enough time for us to end properly. He seemed immensely relieved that I put this to him without being retaliatory or feeling
diminished by his persistent devaluation of me. He said that he
would try to attend regularly in June and July, after his final art
examination, but if he found he was not able to, he would come
back in the autumn to do it properly. I pointed out that sooner or
later he would have to register the pain involved in separating.

In the meantime Mr P's relationship with Britt had its own
share of complications. Strangely enough, at his first meeting with
Stefan they seemed more like accomplices than rivals (Khan,
1979). Both had been intrigued to meet each other. Mr P was surprised and disarmed to hear Stefan's spontaneous confession,
which mirrored his own longing to know what his rival was like.
Stefan admitted that in a dream he had wanted to kill Mr P but
only succeeded in cutting some buttons off his shirt. Not surprisingly, Mr P, for his part, could feel no anger and said, moreover,
that if the two of them had so much in common, they would
merge and gang up against Britt. In fact, the meeting had lasted 5
hours, during which they had gone from pub to pub, getting
drunk together, until they were interrupted by an angry Britt who
was due to go to a concert with Stefan.

Mr P was incapable, however, of relating to Stefan as an equal.
He needed to invest him with qualities of a strong father who

would claim mother but still retain a loving connection with him. Inevitably, he was disappointed. Gradually realizing that Stefan seemed a reflection of himself and was not someone to be admired and looked up to, he lost interest in him.

Further complications arose when Britt produced a life-size photograph of Stefan naked for the final College art exhibition. I could not fail to notice Mr P's consternation and was left wondering what exactly this aroused in him. Was it a wish for a potent male therapist, we wondered? Wavering between his inability to make a claim on Britt or let go of her, he was equally uncertain whether or not to continue therapy. These conflicts surfaced in his potency when he knew he did not want her and his impotence when he felt needy and dependent, showing the dissociation between mind and body, emotions and sexuality. He had doubts as to whether he and Britt could be creative together or let anything grow between them. During all this time he kept me on the outside, not allowing me to provide anything worthwhile or meaningful to the relationship. He seemed unable to use me as a secure base from which he could explore more satisfying ways of relating to the people around him. As he said, "this seems to be all I'm capable of at present". His ultimate dread was of being left with no one. This, in fact, would have reflected his own early absent mother, a deprivation that was continuously mirrored by his lacking a sense of self.

Towards the end of his therapy Mr P acknowledged how much his life had changed, and he seemed to be on the brink of being able to internalize his parents differently, being less antagonistic and critical of them and realizing that somewhere there may have been a warm loving relationship towards him. At times he also showed signs of valuing me and our work together by saying how much his life had changed and recalling how desperate he had been when he first came into therapy. This attitude was, however, not reflected in his treatment of me at this later stage of therapy, when he was often dismissive. Was ending therapy at that point about flight, or was it possible to salvage some integration? Both his choice of Britt and his decision to leave therapy raised the question whether he could value an object that was *there*.

Mr P had always expressed anxiety as to the outcome of his therapy—throughout the years he had wondered what the end would be. Would he ever manage to get out of his narcissistic state, where he felt compelled to distance himself or treat objects badly? Would he be able to stay in a developing relationship, experiencing conflicts and struggling with them? He did seem to have shown some improvement and was more connected to the external world by virtue of his success at work and through his more superficial relationships. For a very long time he had been totally in love with the idea of aesthetics and lost objects; for example, for a couple of years he pursued an obsessive project that involved photographing family graves in a London cemetery. He expended energy on creating a glorified image of himself, and we had to concentrate on dealing with reality in his therapy and his difficulty of relating there. Part of him really wanted to relate and wanted me to be interested in him so that he could bring more of himself into his therapy, but another part was very frightened of the closeness that this would entail. During his therapy he did have moments of genuine awareness of the other person, but he still used destructive splitting to a great extent. This was apparent in the way he attacked the couple (me and himself) with the missed sessions and the way he had intruded between Stefan and Britt. The anger and rejection were parcelled out and moved around between the protagonists, but at base he was the baffled child, left outside the couple. His way of ending therapy was typical of Mr P. I felt that our work was not complete, but, true to form, he showed me his urgent need for attachment but made sure that no one could meet his need. Thus, he slid away from me, and I was left feeling that it was unsatisfactory.

Mr P's ending of therapy

Mr P cut down his time of ending to 7 sessions, after which he was going abroad on holiday with Britt. Although he had left us rather little time, we immediately started the work of reviewing the course of his therapy. In one of his earliest sessions with me, Mr P had remarked that everything he embarked on was "temporary", and I remarked that he still seemed to choose elusive options. Despite the fact that Stefan had ended the relationship with Britt and had another girl-friend, Britt and Stefan seemed to have retained a wistful attachment and were still frequently in touch. Whilst Mr P felt relieved that Stefan was out of the way and hopeful that he could build on what he had with Britt, it was still conditional, and Britt announced that she would review her stay in London at the beginning of the following year. Perhaps they would spend time travelling together, perhaps they would move in together in London, perhaps she would return to Sweden. The rivalry between them was, at times, very destructive. He was furious because he had helped her with her art and she had a lot of success with it. He could have kicked himself for not pursuing his own work. I remarked that his need to keep Britt happy seemed more an attempt to keep the mother inside himself contented and well at any price in the hope that she would recognize him. He replied that in spite of all the difficulties with Britt he had never before felt that he could give the whole of himself to someone.

His last session was both telling and moving. He came an hour late for his session, having confused the time. He brought a huge bunch of irises. I felt, as I was free, that we needed to have a session to conclude his therapy. I pointed out his ambivalence about ending. Perhaps he would have preferred to deposit the flowers on the doorstep and go without a session, because saying goodbye seemed too painful. Mr P said he was utterly amazed that he had got the time wrong, as he had consciously thought that he was not going to miss his last session for anything, no matter what else happened that day. However, he knew that he had shut down on feelings because there was too much feeling there. I reminded him how he had retained his attachment to me even when it was difficult, and he had stayed away from sessions; I told him that I felt sure he would continue to do so in my absence. He said he would remember the not coming to sessions as well as the coming.

He seemed to have more of a sense of who I was and to be able to hold on to the idea that I would still be there even after he had left therapy. He replied that even *he* would not be able to eradicate the eight years of our work together. He said that what he would miss most was the sense of overview I gave him, the different perspective, the words and the ability to look at his situation more objectively. Mr P said he could not imagine never seeing my consulting-room again, nor my dog resting in the hall, nor the plants or the box of tissues. I commented that it felt as if he were like an adolescent leaving home, on the brink of life, ready to find his own base and to explore his own identity in terms of work and relationships. He responded with humour that although he was 35, he had never had a home of his own, and that was the next thing on his agenda, for he was ready to choose his own wallpaper and carpets.

The session ended. We said our goodbyes, and I wished him well. Mr P left rather awkwardly, thanking me and saying that he would no doubt be in touch by sending me invitations to all his exhibitions.

Conclusion

As a result of his intensive psychotherapy treatment over a number of years, Mr P has worked through some aspects of the splitting that is inherent in the narcissistic solution. This splitting was caused by an attempt to maintain an idealization of his emotionally elusive mother, who was unable to contain him. He has now worked through the disappointment of having such a mother and is consequently able to experience a degree of separateness and some integration, enabling him to work productively and to relate better to others. These are at best partial solutions, some of which may not have the solid foundations of permanent change.

This chapter tries to show how psychotherapeutic treatment can make a patient more conscious of his angry feelings towards the early mother, thus reducing the need to idealize her. To some extent, this awareness frees him to use his conflict more constructively. The result will lie somewhere between object-relating and purely narcissistic relating. As Kohut (1984) realized, perhaps this is all that can realistically be expected of narcissistic patients.

CHAPTER FIVE

The move from object-relating to object-usage: a clinical example

Sue Johnson

My attempt to conceptualize my work with a young woman has led me to examine Winnicott's "Use of an Object" concept (1971a). Put simply, the possibility of object-usage results from the exercise of the subject's destructive drive against the object, which enables him to recognize the object as both separate from himself and reliably present in the world; it is dependent upon the object's survival. Until this has been achieved, object-usage is not possible.

In the therapeutic relationship, the patient cannot "use" the therapist until he has experienced the full force of his destructive drive towards the therapist and the therapist has survived and not retaliated. It is this that places the therapist outside the omnipotent control of the patient, and therefore enables the patient to experience "ME" and "NOT-ME". This eventually facilitates in the patient the capacity to "use" that which is "NOT-ME" (Winnicott, 1950–55).

In this account I intend to use clinical material to illustrate the stages in this process and to demonstrate the importance of stating the concept from the patient's point of view, as opposed to that of the therapist.

Winnicott's statement that the concept of object-usage involves a rewriting of the theory of the roots of aggression (1971a) prompted me to review a number of his earlier papers in order to learn how he had arrived at this understanding.

Winnicott wrote at least four papers specifically on aggression and destruction and elaborated his thinking in numerous other papers. Before giving clinical material, I will comment briefly on sections of Winnicott's earlier papers, which contain aspects of his thinking about aggression and destruction over a span of 30 years prior to his eventual formulation of the concept of object-usage in 1971.

The first of these papers, "Aggression" (1939), was written for teachers. In it Winnicott traces the origins of the infant's aggression to appetite or greed, the aim of which is "gratification, peace of mind and body" (p. 171). There is no intended cruelty or danger in the original appetite, although the eventual task for the individual will be to acknowledge the cruelty and greed in the personality in order to be able to sublimate them.

In his second paper on aggression, "Aggression in Relation to Emotional Development" (1950–55), Winnicott links aggression with motility and activity. He makes his point vividly: "A baby kicks in the womb; it cannot be assumed that he is trying to kick his way out" (p. 204). He says that the kicking and biting movements of the infant are not in themselves aggressive, as there is no integration of the personality yet, and therefore no capacity for taking responsibility. He then extends this to patients who in ill health may display aggressiveness without intention. I believe that Winnicott's use of the word "display" is crucial, and I hope to show in this account how I misinterpreted a "display" of aggression for "actual aggression", which would include integration of the personality and intention.

Further on in the same paper Winnicott breaks aggression down into the various stages of ego development:

Early	Pre-integration
	Purpose without concern
Intermediate	Integration
	Purpose with concern
	Guilt

Total personal   Inter-personal relationships
Triangular situations, etc.
Conflict, conscious and unconscious
[Winnicott, 1950–55, pp. 205–206]

He goes on to develop the intermediate "stage of concern" before
moving onto sections on the very early roots of aggression and the
external nature of objects. The root of the "use of an object" concept is clear in this paper in the following sentence:

. . . in the early stages, when the *ME* and the *NOT-ME* are
being established, it is the aggressive component that more
surely drives the individual to a need for a *NOT-ME* or an
object that is felt to be *external*. [Winnicott, 1950–55, p. 215]

Winnicott's paper, "Aggression, Guilt and Reparation" (1960a), is
a development of his "stage of concern" in his previous paper,
which he relates to Klein's "depressive position". His contention
in this paper is that an individual can tolerate the destructive aim
in early loving if he already has evidence of a constructive aim to
refer to, and again he links "health" with the degree of integration
of the personality and the capacity for taking responsibility.
Winnicott states:

Integration is a word that comes in here, because if one can
conceive of a fully integrated person, then that person takes
full responsibility for all feelings and ideas that belong to being alive. By contrast, it is a failure of integration when we
need to find the things we disapprove of outside ourselves
and do so at a price—this price being the loss of the destructiveness which really belongs to ourselves. [Winnicott, 1960a,
p. 82]

Further on I show how my interpretation of a patient's anger
when she was in a state of pre-integration was, in fact, a projection
of my own anger, which arose from my experience of feeling attacked by her.
In "Roots of Aggression" (1964), Winnicott stresses the importance of the stage in early development in which the mother takes
the infant from the belief in magical creation and destruction to
the recognition of a world that exists outside his magical control.

It is this stage that he develops further in his paper, "The Use of an Object and Relating through Identifications":

> Object-relating is an experience of the subject that can be described in terms of the subject as an isolate. When I speak of the use of an object, however, I take object-relating for granted, and add new features that involve the nature and the behaviour of the object. For instance, the object, if it is to be used, must necessarily be real in the sense of being part of shared reality, not a bundle of projections. It is this, I think that makes for the world of difference that there is between relating and usage. [Winnicott, 1971b, p. 88]

I am here principally interested in Winnicott's conception of the early stage of aggression—that of pre-integration—and a technical difficulty I encountered when working in this area. In the clinical example that follows, I illustrate the movement from relating to usage that came about following repeated transference re-enactment in the treatment of a young woman whom I have been seeing for six and a half years on a two-session-a-week basis. After giving a brief history, I discuss only material relevant to the theme of object-usage.

Clinical example

JOANNE

At the time of referral, Joanne was 23 years old. She had had a breakdown during a course and had been admitted to the psychiatric ward of the local hospital. She had picked a hole in her forehead and another one in her arm. Following her discharge from hospital, she had returned home and was living with her parents. She had been offered no further treatment by the hospital. A family relative contacted a psychiatrist privately, who then referred Joanne to me.

The referring psychiatrist said that when she first met Joanne, she thought she was schizophrenic. However, during the course of their meeting she modified her diagnosis from schizophrenia to late adolescent disturbance. I spent some time talking with the referrer about possibilities of adolescent centres and therapeutic communities where Joanne might be seen, as she fell within the age group of the adolescent centre where I worked at that time. In principle, I believed that adolescents were best seen in institutional settings. The referrer thought Joanne needed to be seen individually in a private setting, and she had discussed the referral with Joanne's father, who was willing to pay for her treatment. With serious misgivings, I agreed to see her.

I spoke to Joanne briefly on the telephone to arrange an initial appointment. After I put the telephone down I was surprised to find that I felt a flash of fury. I was confused and puzzled by my reaction, as I could not account for my response in a way that made sense to me.

Searles says the following about mental states of perplexity and confusion:

> I believe that all these states represent a striving to keep out of awareness an intensity, or a type, of affect which is sensed as intolerable to the ego—as threatening to overwhelm the ego and disrupt the interpersonal relatedness. In essence, these states are considered for the purposes of this paper to function as defences against the awareness of repressed affects. [Searles, 1952, p. 70]

On meeting Joanne, my immediate impression was that she was a neglected and frightened waif. The *Shorter Oxford English Dictionary* defines "waif" as "a person who is without home or friends; one who lives uncared-for; an outcast; an unowned or neglected child" (p. 2496).

Joanne's appearance was unkempt and her manner confused and chaotic. She was withdrawn for most of the initial interview. She was barely able to speak and gave me the briefest of details about how she had come to see me. She did, however, give me one vital piece of information—in a timid and questioning voice, she told me that she made people furious.

Joanne appeared to me to be exceedingly vulnerable, and my countertransference was a protective one and it continued to be so for many months. Although I had experienced fury following our telephone conversation, I did not feel remotely furious in my meeting with Joanne. My use of the word "remotely" suggests that, in Searles' terms, I had to defend myself against my feelings of fury, which, at this stage, would threaten to render me unable to work with Joanne.

During the first year of Joanne's treatment she found it difficult to settle herself and to make herself comfortable in my consulting-room. To give the reader an idea of what it was like to be in the room with her, I will describe in some detail her behaviour at the beginning of sessions.

Joanne would slowly and hesitantly make her way across the consulting-room to the chair and would perch on the edge of the chair with her coat on. After a matter of minutes she would place her hands on the arms of chair, then slowly spread her fingers apart in order to grip the arms of the chair. She would then back herself into the chair and shift her position until she could turn her head to the left enough so that she could just about see out of the window behind her out of the corner of her eye. Then she would slowly turn back away from the window, put her head down, and lift her gaze enough to catch a glimpse of me furtively through her dishevelled hair. She would then reposition herself and repeat the process, turning her head to the right and studying my books on the bookcase beside her. She would then resume her original position and scan around the room, and finally she would look up and around the ceiling. All of this took some considerable time and energy—each movement was made cautiously and painstakingly. Each time Joanne came to a session it was as though she was entering a completely foreign territory that had to be gone over with the precision of a sniffer dog, lest an unexploded bomb was lying undetected.

Joanne thus spent a significant portion of each session simply trying to make herself relatively comfortable—I say "relatively" because I do not believe she was ever really comfortable. I, too, felt uncomfortable and was initially very tense during her sessions—I found her behaviour at the beginning of sessions excruciating to behold. Both she and I were acutely aware of the slightest sound—either inside or outside the house. When she had finally managed to get herself into a somewhat more relaxed position, I was keen not to "disturb" her. If I shifted in my chair or tried to speak, she jumped.

My experience of myself in relation to Joanne's behaviour was that I was a persecuting, terrifying monster. At the same time, I felt controlled by her behaviour and kept at a distance from her. I also felt myself kept from being able to interpret what was going on between us. I felt badly about my capacities as a therapist. These are statements from my experience.

From Joanne's point of view, I believe that she was simply acquainting herself with the environment while at the same time attempting to protect herself from me. Of course, she was left impoverished, but at this stage it was shelter, not food, that she needed most.

Two of Winnicott's diagrams in "Psychoses and Child Care" (1952b) visually represent what was taking place between Joanne and me during this time. Winnicott writes:

> Figs. 9 and 10 represent the way in which the individual is affected by environmental tendencies, especially at a very early stage. Fig. 9 shows how, by active adaptation to the child's needs, the environment enables him to be in undisturbed isolation. The infant does not know. In this state he makes a spontaneous movement and the environment is dis-

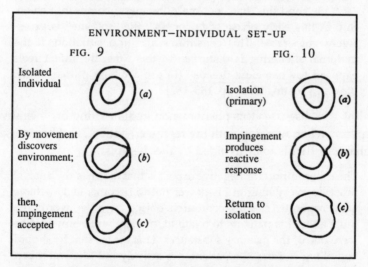

covered without loss of sense of self. Fig. 10 shows faulty adaptation to the child, resulting in impingement of the environment so that the individual must become a reactor to this impingement. The sense of self is lost in this situation and is only regained by a return to isolation. [Winnicott, 1952, pp. 222–223]

As in Fig. 9(b), Joanne was discovering her environment, but any movement on my part or any unexpected sound produced a reactive response on hers, as in Fig. 10(b).

Tustin discussed "primary integrations" in the following manner:

> Work with unintegrated and disintegrated states in children has led me to think that one of the earliest integrations which needs to take place is between "hard" and "soft" sensations. In the sensation-dominated state of early infancy the infant's primary distinctions are between "comfort" and "discomfort" —"pleasure" and "unpleasure". "Soft" sensations are pleasurable and comfortable. "Hard" sensations are unpleasurable and uncomfortable. . . . In *Beyond the Pleasure Principle*, Freud (1920) alerted us to the process of *projection* by which uncomfortable states are felt outside the body. "Comfort" is "me"— "Discomfort" is "not-me." "Softness" is "me", "hardness" is "not-me". This is well illustrated by a commonly reported feature of psychotic children, many of whom will only eat soft foods and reject hard lumps. With this dichotomy between the "soft me" and the "hard not-me", "twoness" comes into being. But, in this early phase of "twoness", the "soft me" is excessively vulnerable. This constitutes a critical situation. If the maternal sheltering is disturbed at this time, the infant feels exposed to "nameless dreads" (to use a telling phrase of Dr. Bion's). [Tustin, 1981, pp. 185–187]

Balint also discusses this phenomenon in his writing on "negative aspects" when working with the regressed patient, and he stresses behaviour that is to be avoided by the therapist:

> The other important negative aspect is that at times the analyst must do everything in his power not to become, or to behave as, a separate, sharply-contoured object. In other words, he must allow his patients to relate to, or exist with, him as if he were one of the primary substances. This means that he should be willing to carry the patient, not actively but like water carries the swimmer or the earth carries the walker, that is, to be there for the patient, to be used without too much resistance against being used. [M. Balint, 1968, p. 167]

One day during this period of Joanne's treatment I was walking my dogs through woods not far from my house. I came upon a small, young rabbit that had clearly been startled by the dogs rushing past. The rabbit was frozen to the spot, so that I almost did not see it. I stopped in my tracks. The rabbit and I remained motionless, staring at each other for a matter of seconds—the rabbit scared to run, I hesitant to move lest I frighten it further and thereby attract the attention of the dogs, who would have delighted in chasing it.

In a subsequent session with Joanne that moment came back to me, and I related the story to her and said that it reminded me of the way she and I behaved with each other. She responded by keeping her head down and smiling very faintly.

I arranged to see Joanne at the end of my working sessions, as I felt exhausted and in need of a break after her sessions. Winnicott states:

> I have recently been struck by the following idea, derived from clinical work, that when a patient is engaged in discovering the aggressive root the analyst is more exhausted by the process, one way or another, than when the patient is discovering the erotic root of the instinctual life. [Winnicott, 1950–55, p. 214]

During the course of the first year of Joanne's treatment my concern about her being at risk increased significantly. My fears for her safety were confirmed when I learned from her GP (who had learned from Joanne's sister) that a man had exposed himself to her. When I tried to enquire about this, Joanne told me she had been walking home alone from the station at about midnight. She also told me she had been crossing a large open piece of land near my house to get to her sessions, but she had recently changed her route.

Shortly after this incident, Joanne became very distressed in a session and told me she was frightened she would hurt a child. She said she did not want to hurt anyone but was afraid she would. She felt extremely guilty about having these thoughts, made it clear that she hated herself for having them, and believed herself to be full of evil and badness. Furthermore, she was worried about what I might think of her.

I understood this communication to be about Joanne's fears related to experiences she herself had had as a child, and that she was the endangered child who might be hurt, either by me in the treatment or externally by someone else or herself. I continued to believe that twice-weekly treatment was not sufficient to provide the containment necessary for her to begin to explore either her real life experiences or her inner world, and that in order to do this she needed to be away from home and in a residential setting. I feared that she and I might "disturb" something in her that would be uncontainable. At this point I also learned, from both her and her GP, that her parents were putting pressure on her to get a job. I was amazed at their failure to see how ill their daughter was and, with hindsight, believed that by agreeing to see her on a private basis I had unintentionally colluded with their denial of her illness.

With Joanne's agreement—which was in fact simply compliance—and in consultation with her GP and the referring psychiatrist, I made a referral to a therapeutic community.

Initially Joanne seemed to experience some degree of relief and hope at the possibility of being taken seriously and allowed to be ill. She was assessed over a period of months (while I was continuing to see her) but was not offered a place, as it was felt that she "was not taking responsibility" for wishing to change but was going there for punishment. The assessor confirmed my fears that she was at very real risk of suicide. Of course she was not "taking responsibility"—in Winnicott's terms, her personality was not integrated enough for her to have the capacity to take responsibility.

Much later I learned that this referral had been a re-enactment between Joanne and me. Joanne's mother had not wanted Joanne and had returned to work when Joanne was born, leaving her in the care of her mother-in-law for most of the time. When Joanne was approximately 18 months old, there had been a row between the parents and the grandmother, and the parents had abruptly moved away, taking Joanne with them. Joanne did not see her grandmother again until her sister was born, when Joanne was 4 years old.

When I referred her to the therapeutic community, I became the rejecting mother in the transference who was wanting to abort Joanne and her treatment. I was also the grandmother who, in phantasy, had sent her away. Of course, the truth was that I had not wanted her when she had been referred to me, because I had believed that twice-weekly treatment would not be suitable for her. I had also intuitively known that work with her would put me in touch with feelings in myself that I would find extremely difficult to tolerate.

The rejection was played out over and over again for the next two years, particularly at the end of sessions and at breaks. Often Joanne would not be ready to speak until the end of the session, and then she would not be ready to go and would go out "in a whirl", as she later called it. She would leave the house, slamming the door and shouting loudly as she went out and down the street that I just wanted to hurt her. On occasions I was aware that neighbours must have been wondering what I was doing to her. At times when she was slightly more contained, she would only mutter under her breath as she went out. The same pattern occurred in relation to breaks—she would begin to talk more as the break approached and then feel even more rejected by the break.

She latched onto the therapeutic community's phrase—"not taking responsibility"—and used this to blame herself for the state she was in. She protested that she was evil and that she had to take responsibility for her evilness. She said that at the community parents who hurt children were treated sympathetically—they were not punished but received understanding. She must therefore have done something terribly wrong to deserve punishment rather than understanding—that was how she understood their rejection of her, as well as mine. Although I attempted to interpret the punishment she experienced when I referred her there, it was a meaningless communication. It was meaningless because, at this point, I was unable to own my rage towards her. Intellectually I knew the interpretation to make, but I was unable to cathect it emotionally. In addition, if I made any interpretation that carried with it the implication of ego-integration—that is, if I spoke to her as though she were a whole person—she heard this as evidence that I, too, blamed her. I now believe that these interpretations were actually punishing on my part—they were expressions of my rage, which I still did not know about. Joanne knew about my rage with her long before I did—in fact, as soon as we met, she had warned me that I would feel it if I worked with her!

Searles writes about the defensive aspect of incorporative processes in the transference–countertransference relationship. His work with a patient mirrors my experience with Joanne:

> This stalemate changed rapidly and promptly into one of relatively free interaction between the patient and me as soon as I was able to recognize in myself a quite intense degree of anger towards him. Although I expressed it quite directly to him on more than one occasion, the important ingredient was that I had become able to feel it very strongly and without attendant anxiety. Previously, I had been aware of feeling exceedingly tense, but not of feeling angry. [Searles, 1951, p. 67]

Sometimes Joanne and I would be merged as one during the sessions. At other times she would be the frightened child and I the violent adult. Then it would switch. She would hit herself on the chair, bang her arms, and shout at herself. At those times she was being the violent and frightening adult to herself, and I was she—the helpless child who could only watch what was being done to her and who did not know what would happen next. My panic about what to do to stop her meant that I was unable to think. When I tried to speak, she jumped violently and became terrified of me, and then I became the violent adult in the transference and she resumed the position of the frightened child. The transference shifted abruptly from one minute to the next, as she moved from one persecuting position to another in her inner world, so that I had difficulty keeping up with it. In his paper on aggression, Winnicott states:

> If destruction there (in the inner world) is excessive and unmanageable, very little reparation is possible and we can do nothing to help. All that the child can do is either to deny ownership of bad fantasies or to dramatise them. [Winnicott, 1939, p. 172]

In order to give the reader a picture of my state of mind during this phase in the treatment, I will quote from notes I made following one of our sessions.

After Joanne left, mind in a panic—what to do—write a letter, make telephone calls, do something for myself—felt persecuted—had to go to the word processor. Surprised that she left and didn't bang the front door—she left better—I had the panic.

Didn't know where to put myself in the session—falling asleep, trying to keep awake, just wanted to get the session over with—wanted the end of the sleepiness—wanted to end the overwhelming sense of—what is it—tiredness, exhaustion, feeling drained, helplessness, etc.

It is terrible to see her hurting herself—I said something about the fact that I had to take responsibility for the fact that I had hurt her by referring her elsewhere. I feel I should be able to stop her. I tried to say to her that she could only express her anger with me by hurting herself. I can't get this clear enough in my mind to interpret it properly to her. I feel so fused with her at the time (in the sessions) that I can't think clearly enough—I just want to go to sleep.

The reader can see the chaos I experienced both during and following the sessions and the way in which I tried to use my word processor to help me process my experience.

One day Joanne hurled her bag across the consulting-room and then threw herself violently into the corner of the room and began hitting herself and banging her arms on the floor. I felt unable to witness her behaviour and told her to stop it. She continued, and eventually I got up and went over to her. I spoke to her as though I were speaking to a child who was misbehaving, and I told her to go back and sit in the chair. At that moment she became frightened of me and cowered from me, no doubt because she could hear anger in my voice. I realized that she was actually frightened of me, and I asked her to come back to her chair and I put out my hand to her. She initially reacted as though she thought I was going to hit her, but when she looked up and saw that I had my hand out rather than up to hit her, she got up and returned to her chair. Both she and I were visibly taken aback, surprised and shaken.

Searles says:

Uncomfortable though it is for the therapist to feel afraid of the murderous patient, it is still harder for him to realize the full extent of his own murderousness towards the patient, and to see that the latter is unaware of feeling murderous and is experiencing, instead, intense fear of the therapist who is viewed as murderously insane. It is more acceptable to the therapist's superego to feel intimidated than intimidating, and the realization that the patient is deathly afraid of one tends, at least initially, to weaken one's own feeling of control over one's rage. [Searles, 1961, p. 534]

I have no memory of what I said on the occasion described earlier which prompted Joanne to throw herself into the corner. My current understanding is that, at that moment, she was dramatizing behaviour that she had witnessed and felt she had provoked, without knowing how she had done it. Much later she remembered an event when she was a young child—her mother had run out of the family home screaming and shouting down the street, and Joanne had not known whether or not she would return.

Winnicott states:

This thing that there is in between relating and use is the subject's placing of the object outside the area of the subject's omnipotent control; that is, the subject's perception of the object as an external phenomenon, not as a projective entity, in fact recognition of it as an entity in its own right.

This change (from relating to usage) means that the subject destroys the object. . . . Without the experience of maximum destructiveness (object not protected) the subject never places the analyst outside and therefore can never do more than experience a kind of self-analysis, using the analyst as a projection of a part of the self. . . . The essential feature is the analyst's survival and the intactness of the psychoanalytic technique. [Winnicott, 1971a, p. 89–92]

My behaviour in the above episode may be termed "countertransference acting out": I did not remain in my chair and try to interpret what was happening. It could also be termed "a behavioural interpretation". During the moment when I had my hand out to Joanne, I was clearly outside her omnipotent control and an object in my own right. My behaviour did not fit with her illusion—I was not going to hit her. In a subsequent session I was able to make a verbal interpretation, which Joanne could then hear:

When I acted to stop you hurting yourself, I intervened in the violence in your family, as you needed someone to do when you were a child.

Following this, Joanne began to test out whether or not she could "use" me. For the next two years she wrote to me between sessions and used her letters to contain her destructive impulses. She wrote about her badness and evilness, about wanting to cut herself or commit suicide, rather than acting on those impulses. I did not reply in writing to her letters but always had her most recent letter sitting on the bookcase beside me at the beginning of the session and often began the session by thanking her for her letter and by referring to its contents. She always looked on the bookcase as soon as she entered the room to see whether her letter had arrived. The letters could be seen as having actually provided Joanne with the additional sessions she was in need of—she was able to express material in her letters that she was not able to express in her sessions. I, too, had time to process the material in her letters before seeing her. She ceased behaving in a self-destructive way in her sessions and instead used her sessions to talk about those impulses. She moved from picking the hole in her forehead (which I learned much later had been there since she was a very young child) and hitting and bruising herself as she began to behave in what appeared to be a "destructive" way towards me and the psychotherapeutic setting.

It is usually my practice to greet my patients at the front door and to see them into my house, but to let them see themselves out of my consulting-room and my house. One day Joanne slammed the consulting-room door (as she had on a number of occasions) and then crashed and banged around loudly in the hall before she went out. I could, of course, hear the racket she was making, and after she left I emerged from my consulting-room to find the hall littered with the coats and hats from the coat rack, which was now empty. My initial experience was one of shock—with a marked absence of feeling. It took some minutes before I felt both furious and distressed.

In the following session I tried to interpret what I believed to be Joanne's anger with me for failing to contain her in the sessions and said that I would see her out of the door in future. Although she continued to shout at me on many occasions, I was there at the door to receive it.

Some time later Joanne again started to slam the consulting-room door as she went out—but this time I was behind her, and I grabbed it as she started to slam it. She immediately said: "I'm sorry." I said: "No, you're not . . . you're angry." (The reader can clearly see that the person who was angry was me!) Joanne be-came very distressed at this. She said she wasn't angry—she was sorry. I said: "Yes, I know you're sorry . . . but at that moment you were very angry with me because it was the end of the session . . . you were furious . . . but as soon as you realized it, you were sorry. You were so afraid of feeling angry that the moment you felt it you were sorry for it."

In the above example, my interpretation to Joanne was a straightforward one based on encounter with the reality principle, but the interpretation carries with it the assumption that Joanne was functioning as a "whole person", that her ego was integrated enough at that moment for her to experience anger. Now I believe that she was in an infantile rage. The interpretation was from my point of view, not from hers—I was telling her what my experi-ence was and what I believed she felt!

During this time in Joanne's treatment I was dealing with her as best I could, and she was doing her best to communicate with me, but it is painful to recall the earlier stages in her treatment as I am forced to recognize and accept the inadequacy of my under-standing and technique. At the time, I was frightened of the dam-age I was doing to her as she was in a vulnerable state. In that sense, I was frightened of my own aggression and therefore un-able to interpret in a way that might have contained her. I also experienced her as attacking me, but the point here is that that was something that was going on in me—it was a problem in my transference to her. I deliberately use the word "transference" as opposed to "countertransference" because it was in me and it manifested itself in my countertransference to Joanne. This was part of our "shared reality". I believe that this is what Winnicott was referring to in the following section:

> If I am right in this, then it follows that discussion of the sub-ject of relating is a much easier exercise for analysts than is the

discussion of usage, since relating may be examined as a phenomenon of the subject, and psychoanalysis always likes to be
able to eliminate all factors that are environmental, except in
so far as the environment can be thought of in terms of projective mechanisms. But in examining usage there is no escape:
the analyst must take into account the nature of the object, not
as a projection, but as a thing in itself. [Winnicott, 1971a, p. 88]

When I interpreted Joanne's anger, I was the one who was projecting—I was furious, but I was projecting my fury onto her. Although Joanne's behaviour appeared to be an expression of anger,
at this stage it could not be counted as such, because she was not
yet integrated enough to be able to experience anger. I am not
suggesting that her behaviour was not "angry behaviour"—that
would be foolish. But I am suggesting that she was still too ill
actually to be able to experience anger and that, therefore, my
interpretation of her anger was technically incorrect. In those moments of illness she was in a state of pre-integration, but when
confronted with me and my anger she feared me and she quickly
functioned in a state of intermediate integration, felt guilty for
what she had done, and apologized.

Joanne and I have recently discussed these episodes. She says
that she knows that they happened, but she cannot remember
them. I believe this is because she was not actually integrated
enough at the time to be there to experience them.

I will quote further from Winnicott:

It will be seen that, although destruction is the word I am
using, this actual destruction belongs to the object's failure to
survive. Without this failure, destruction remains potential.
The word "destruction" is needed, not because of the baby's
impulse to destroy, but because of the object's liability not to
survive, which also means to suffer change in quality, in attitude. [Winnicott, 1971a, p. 93]

He goes on to say that what is required is:

a rewriting of the theory of the roots of aggression since most
of that which has already been written by analysts has been
formulated without reference to that which is being discussed
in this chapter. The assumption is always there, in orthodox
theory, that aggression is reactive to the encounter with the

> reality principle, whereas here it is the destructive drive that
> creates the quality of externality. This is central in the structure
> of my argument . . . *There is no anger* in the destruction of the
> object to which I am referring, though there could be said to be
> joy at the object's survival. From this moment, or arising out of
> this phase, the object is *in fantasy* always being destroyed. This
> quality of "always being destroyed" makes the reality of the
> surviving object felt as such, strengthens the feeling tone, and
> contributes to object-constancy. The object can now be used.
> [Winnicott, 1971a, p. 93]

I believe that Winnicott's phrase "liability not to survive" contains
within it the idea of the potential vulnerability of the therapist.
Today there is a growing awareness and agreement about the inevitability of the therapist's emotional response to the patient at
great depth. At the time of Winnicott's writing, however, there
was an assumption that through their own analyses therapists had
not only achieved, but, furthermore, had remained at, an ad-
vanced stage of development that rendered them immune from
experiencing either moments or phases of regression to states of
pre-integration. It is my experience that unless I am open to re-
experiencing my own states of pre-integration, I am unable to
work in this area of very early disturbance. Furthermore, I am
aware that I have had some of my most meaningful and produc-
tive sessions with patients when I have felt at my most vulnerable.

With the benefit of hindsight and with some distance from the
experience with Joanne that I have described, I realize that I am in
agreement with Winnicott over there being no anger in the destruction of the object. My interpretation of Joanne's anger was
based on her "display" of aggression as a reaction to the encounter with the reality principle, but this understanding was limited. I
do not believe that Joanne actually experienced anger when she
went to slam the door, as she was in Winnicott's "early" stage of
aggressiveness in terms of her ego development—that is, she was
unintegrated at that moment and therefore not able to experience
anger. However, I do believe that she felt sorry. My grabbing the
door (my retaliation) frightened her, and she reacted from the
intermediate stage of aggression, which includes ego-integration
sufficient for the existence of and therefore fear of the talion. I

think that my experience of shock without feeling in reaction to her pulling the hats and coats off the coat rack was the counter-transference counterpart of her absence of aggressive, purposive feeling and that, in both instances cited above, she was in a state of excitement without ego-integration. I believe she did subsequently experience sorrow, as I subsequently experienced both fury and distress.

Although on the face of it Joanne's behaviour may appear aggressive, it takes only a slight shift in perspective to see these episodes as evidence of a lack of ego-integration as a result of "failings" in the containing function of the therapist. I hope it will now be obvious why I deliberately used the word "transference" when speaking of my difficulties with Joanne.

Joanne's "dramatizing" behaviour lessened considerably when eventually I found a way of wording interpretations that contained a recognition of her illness (Winnicott's stage of pre-integration) and thereby made allowance for an absence of intent and responsibility. Those interpretations were more digestible to her.

When my interpretations were not digestible (in Tustin's terms, when they were "hard sensations"), she let me know by flinching or by jerking her head. Those physical reactions appeared to be involuntary. Later in the treatment, when she was more able to talk to me, she would repeat back to me what I had said in a way that alerted me to the way she had heard it, and which then made it possible for me to say it to her in another way. She was subsequently able to accept and use those interpretations to integrate her ego.

An indication that Joanne has begun to rediscover her good maternal object (which I believe was her grandmother) is the fact that for the past 18 months Joanne has been doing residential work in a home for the elderly. She recently described the following episode she had experienced with one of the residents. The resident had to be "turned" every two hours in the night. Joanne went to do this, and the resident thrashed about, kicked, and hit out. Joanne described the resident's behaviour as "frenzied—with an aim, but without knowing what she was doing". Joanne said that although it was necessary for the resident's welfare that she be turned, she thought that when she went to do this, the resident was probably comfortable, and it was then painful for her. All the resident could experience was the painful aspect of being turned; the aim of the frenzy was to stop the pain.

Joanne was clearly communicating that she knew how painful it was to get into a comfortable position eventually, only to be turned out.

* * *

In this account I have tried to examine Winnicott's "Use of an Object" concept within the context of his earlier thinking in the areas of aggression and destruction, and to illustrate through clinical material the movement in the transference from relating to usage. I have concentrated on the pre-integration stage of aggression in ego development and the technical difficulty this presents in interpretation. I have suggested that interpretation of anger, when working with a patient in a state of pre-integration, may be a projection of the therapist's anger.

CHAPTER SIX

The potential for trauma
in the transference
and countertransference

Ruth Berkowitz

In a little-quoted paper, Balint raises questions about Freud's theory of trauma and offers his own views (Balint, 1969). Although the controversy surrounding the question of whether or not the trauma was to be understood only as a consequence of an external event remains an on-going issue, it is not Freud's views that I wish to discuss here but those of Balint. From his paper, entitled "Trauma and Object Relationship", it appears that he considered that there were many difficulties in translating Freud's theory into practice and that this paper was his attempt to look for the missing parts of an incomplete theory.

From clinical experience Balint put forward the following propositions: (1) pathogenically, the most important traumas happen in early childhood; (2) although the original concept of trauma described experiences with unfamiliar objects, it was his view that ". . . psychoanalytic experience invariably showed that there existed a close and intimate relationship between the child and the person who inflicted the trauma on him" (p. 431); and (3) "traumatogenic" objects were primarily oedipal objects or

111

people—for example, nurses, governesses, tutors, educators—who derived their authority from these oedipal objects.

Balint attempted to incorporate these factors into an understanding not only of object relations but also of what he called the "finer dynamics of traumatogenesis" (Balint, 1969). This he described as a three-phase structure underpinned by a necessary condition—namely, that in order to inflict a trauma, a certain intensity of a relationship should exist between the child and the traumatogenic object. The child must be dependent on the adult, and although there may be ambivalence, for the adult to be potentially traumatogenic, the child's relationship to him must be mainly trusting and loving.

(a) *The first phase:* The immature child is dependent on the adult, and although frustrations in their relationship may occur, leading to irritation and even rage at times, the relationship between the child and the adult is essentially trusting.

(b) *The second phase:* In this phase, the adult, contrary to the child's expectations, does something highly exciting, frightening, or painful. This may happen once quite suddenly or repeatedly. Balint gives examples such as the adult not being reliable enough, being preoccupied in other directions and therefore neglectful; he may be prompted by some unconscious drive, and, as Balint points out, dependent people create intensely tempting situations for the release of suppressed drives; or the adult may be frustrated and not able to find gratification because of external circumstances. The danger here is that there may be a mutual seduction, leading to very passionate actions

> which, however, need not be necessarily genital sexual; quite often they amount only to excesses of tenderness or excesses of cruelty, amounting to a severe overstimulation of the child or to completely ignoring the child's approaches which means rejection causing deep disappointment. [M. Balint, 1969, p. 432]

Although this phase, according to Balint "does not always act traumatically", it is very "impressive".

(c) *The third phase:* It is here that the *real completion* of the trauma sets in:

... the child, either having in mind the adult's passionate participation in the events of the second phase, approaches his partner again with a wish and offer to continue the exciting passionate game, or, still in pain and distress about the fact that in the previous phase his approach remained unrecognized, ignored or misunderstood, now tries again to get some understanding recognition and comfort. What happens quite often in either case is a completely unexpected refusal. The adult behaves as if he does not know anything about the previous excitement or rejection; in fact, he acts as if nothing had happened. [p. 433]

This chapter explores how these ideas might apply to the relationship between analyst and patient in the analytic setting and, particularly, considers the view that it is in the *third phase* described by Balint that the real trauma occurs. The *first phase*, as described by Balint, is replayed in the relationship of dependence of the patient on the analyst. The *second phase* occurs in the tendency to repeat the original most painful experience. It is well known that, according to Freud (1920g), some patients, unable to remember certain parts of their past, must act them out in their relationship with their analyst: the repetition compulsion. The analytic setting, in fact, facilitates this. What of *phase three*? It is this phase that concerns Balint. The analyst must not participate in the original excitement, as had the original traumatogenic object, yet if the analyst were to follow Freud's advice that the usual benevolent passive objectivity should be maintained, it would be an enactment of this phase. The analyst must "choose his own behaviour deliberately so that it should be different from the original traumatogenic objects" (M. Balint, 1969, p. 434). Balint asks what this new role might be in order that it could be safely therapeutic and suggests that this may start a new fruitful discussion about analytic technique.

A citation search of the psychoanalytic literature between 1981 and 1997 yielded only six references, two of which were in German, to this paper on trauma by Balint. The purpose here is to consider the work of other writers that may have some bearing on Balint's views, although their thinking may not have been linked to that of Balint or his paper on trauma.

(a) Is there any foundation for considering that an analogy can be drawn between *phase one*, and the relationship between therapist and patient?

(b) What is repeated in *phase two;* what is the role of the therapist in this phase? Does he, like the patient, repeat the original experience, and what advances in thinking might there be to avoid this?

(c) How, in *phase three*, might the recognition of one's role be understood in the analytic process in relation to Balint's view that failure to recognize one's role in a traumatic experience seals the trauma?

The potential for trauma in the analytic setting

In Balint's paper he draws a parallel between the trauma in the child's early life and that which might occur in the analytic setting.

The first phase

As Balint suggests, to inflict a trauma there should be a certain intensity in the relationship between the child patient and traumatogenic object, and the relationship should be essentially trusting. The setting in psychoanalytic psychotherapy contributes to the experience of safety and trust, and, as Klauber (1986) points out, much is done by the setting and the psychoanalytic arrangements to contain and reduce trauma from the start, thereby perhaps engendering a sense of trust. Klauber says, however, that we may underrate the drastic nature of what we do, in spite of there being arrangements as well as interpretation to contain and reduce the trauma from the start. He alludes to the intensity of the experience in his use of the phrase that the patient may feel that the analyst is "jet-propelled" into magical status, and he even goes as far as to suggest that the early experience of the analytic setting may itself be traumatic (Klauber, 1986). In his paper he uses two of Freud's definitions of traumatic situations: "an experience of helplessness on the part of the ego in the face of accumulation of excitation whether of external or internal origin" (Freud, 1926d [1925]), and, "a breach in an otherwise efficacious barrier against stimuli" (Freud, 1920g). The breach in analysis is of the barrier against the excitation of unconscious phantasy and unconscious memory. Rosenfeld (1987) echoes this when he says that it is important to remember how strong an influence the analyst can have on the patient.

The second phase

As mentioned earlier, two aspects seem significant in this phase:

(a) the nature of the repetition compulsion and the extent to which the therapist is drawn into this repetition; and

(b) the participation by the therapist in a repetition compulsion that is like that of the earlier object.

It was Freud's view that the patient is "obliged to *repeat* the repressed material as a contemporary experience instead of, as the physician would prefer to see, *remembering* it as something belonging to the past" (Freud, 1920g, p. 18). What is striking about these repetitions is that it is not only pleasurable experiences that are being repeated but that "the compulsion to repeat also includes from the past experiences which include no possibility of pleasure, and which can never, even long ago, have brought satisfaction even to instinctual impulses which have since been repressed" (p. 20). Looked at more closely, the repetition of earlier unwanted situations and painful emotions is the repetition of an object relationship. Freud says that patients seek to

revive them (painful experiences) with the greatest ingenuity. They seek to bring about the interruption of the treatment while it is still incomplete; they contrive once more to feel themselves scorned, to oblige the physician to speak severely to them and treat them coldly . . . [p. 20]

Although Freud was talking of unwanted situations and painful emotions, others do consider the experience in terms of trauma. Bollas, for example, suggests that these "traumatic" conditions are the very circumstances in which the patient is *"entering the intrinsically traumatic in the process of analysis, unconsciously asking that the trauma of things done be addressed"* (Bollas, 1995, p. 113).

The thinking in this area seems to have developed from the idea of the patient bringing pressure to bear on the therapist to collude in the repetition compulsion, through to ideas about the therapist's own contribution to this experience and, further, to a recognition that both play a significant part. Several authors describe this intense pressure put on therapists in a variety of ways, by pushing and prodding (Sandler, 1976) or through intensive projective identification (Brenman-Pick, 1985; Joseph, 1985). Rosenfeld (1987) describes the latter experience vividly:

> Unconsciously, he (the patient) often tries to involve the analyst in his experiences by very forceful projections, sometimes so violent that they appear to be attacks on the analyst and his work. This is a painful and difficult situation for any analyst to bear. [p. 36]

Later on he says:

> I believe that the repetition of early infantile states is one of the most important factors in treating transference and countertransference entanglements . . . the patient tries to escape the unbearable anxiety that pervades his analytic experience. The repetition takes place, of course, via very intense projective identification. In this way the unbearable anxiety is both communicated and projected into the analyst in the analysis. [pp. 273–274]

Baker (1993) writes in a similar way about what he calls the "dangers of countertransference acting out":

> Although it is apparent that a rejection is being invited, and in fact the patient is insisting that the analyst becomes and is indeed a transference object, i.e. replica by role in the here-and-now of the "rejecting" parent of the past, the truth is that this is precisely what the patient dreads since that trauma would be a clear repetition of the one that caused the original damage. [p. 1227]

The handling of such problems is not easy, and countertransference acting out is sometimes inevitable, even in the most experienced hands. Baker himself suggests that the more ill or damaged the patient, the less he will be able to experience the analyst as a new object. He also suggests that too much work in the transference may prevent the patient from seeing the analyst as a new object.

The consequences of this repetition by the therapist have been described by both Rosenfeld (1987) and Baker (1993) as potential impasses—indeed, failures—and they imply that these impasses are not "blamed" on the patient and his psychopathology but attributed to the factors within the analyst to which the patient was responding. Rosenfeld is sensitive to the experience of the patient in the analytic situation and to the potential for humiliation within it, for example in feeling small or put down, or that the analyst understands the patient so much better than the patient does himself. He describes several situations in which the analyst may contribute to the impasse as well as considering traumatic experiences in the analysis. The analyst, because of the violence of the projection of these anxieties, may react with feelings of being attacked and may become irritated and resentful. Rosenfeld also talks in this context about the dangers of treating thin-skinned patients—those who are hypersensitive and easily hurt in everyday life and analysis—as though they are thick-skinned. They may be brought near to collapse, particularly if the destructive aspects of patients' behaviour are constantly repeated in analytic interpretations. He cautions that these thin-skinned patients are fundamentally traumatized and vulnerable, and mistakes may add to their trauma—mistakes that, he says, are very difficult to remedy afterwards. There are risks attached not only to negative countertransference responses but also to positive intentions or desire to do well. This is particularly dangerous when the patient's psychopathology creates strain in the countertransference. Severely traumatized patients who are often driven to repeat past traumatic situations in the analytic situation are particularly likely to draw the analyst into unconscious collusions. These situations are, of course, extremely painful to the analyst, and if they are unbearable, the analyst may collude by creating corrective therapeutic experiences. Baker (1993) also considers the question of avoiding what he calls the "countertransference acting out". He quotes the work of King (1978) and her understanding of negative reaction as a communication—the only way the patient has to convey the feelings, for example, of rejection and uselessness. While the therapist may well be drawn into the repetition by the powerful invitation, as described by Baker (1993), amongst others, some authors have gone further in their understanding of the therapist's contribution to this experience and consider other aspects of the analyst's response beyond its reflection of aspects of the patient. Money-Kyrle (1955), for example, describes aspects of the analyst's self that might be evoked, such as superego anxieties, not understanding, or guilt. Brenman-Pick (1985) comments that some patients touch off in the analyst deep issues and anxieties relating to the need to be loved and the fear of catastrophic consequences in the face of the analyst's perception of his own defects.

In a paper entitled "Not Everything Is Projective Identification", Sandler draws attention to aspects of analytic functioning that he calls a

> chart-making facility that provides us with numbers of maps we use but do not know we are using . . . (which) enter into the way in which we organize our individual perception of the world, and indeed organize our own specific personalities. [Sandler, 1993, p. 1099]

He goes on to quote the view of Jacobs (1993) that the analytic process involves the interplay of two psychologies, that the inner experience of the analyst often provides a valuable pathway to understanding the inner experiences of the patient, and that, not infrequently, the analytic progress depends on the working-through of resistances in the analyst as well as in the patient. According to Jacobs, our ability to understand another person depends on our capacity to listen not only to that individual but to ourselves as well.

Racker (1968) elaborates in greater detail this idea of there being two personalities in the analytic relationship. He says that the analytic situation is

> an interaction between two personalities, in both of which the ego is under pressure from the id, the superego and the external world; each personality has its internal and external dependencies, anxieties and pathological defenses; each is also a child with its internal parents; and each of these whole person-

alities—that of the analysand and that of the analyst—responds to every event of the analytic situation. [Racker, 1968, p. 180]

This recognition of the more personal idiosyncratic reactions as having to do primarily with the analyst's own concerns and with unconscious aspects of his mind could be seen as a step towards what might be termed a more subjective approach.

What was not yet acknowledged in these ideas, however, was the possibility that the patient might be responding to the subjective experience of the analyst, conveyed in many ways, both verbally and non-verbally. Racker (1968) addresses this point by saying that the "analysis of the patient's fantasies about countertransference which in the widest sense constitute the causes and consequence of the transference, is an essential part of the analysis of transferences" (p. 131).

That is, not only does the patient bring his earlier experiences to the analysis, but he also responds to the way in which the analyst responds to his material—as conveyed by the following vignette:

JANE

Jane, a 16-year-old adolescent, began her therapy with what felt like missiles being fired at me. Her superior and contemptuous attitude showed itself in withering comments about my interpretations, about the setting, about therapy. I felt ashamed and stupid, and after the first week found myself wondering whether I would buckle under the strain. I understood this as a communication to me about the strain she felt she had been under most of her life, burdened with unrealistic expectations, which, she felt, were to gratify her parents' needs. I also came to realize that she was trying to discover for herself whether I would buckle. Generally at the end she left the session hurriedly and without saying goodbye. One day when she had spent the whole session belittling me, I ended by saying that perhaps it was frightening to her when she spoke in this way. She strode slowly to the door and looked at me, as though to find out how I had really reacted. "See you", she said.

Some thirty years earlier, Ferenczi "had come to the conclusion that the patients have an exceedingly refined sensitivity to the wishes, tendencies, whims, sympathies and antipathies of their analyst even if the analyst is completely unaware of this sensitivity" (Ferenczi, 1931, p. 158).

It would seem that for quite some time analysts have remained unaware of this sensitivity in the patient, and it is only more recently that the patient's curiosity about the mind of the analyst has been of interest. As Aron points out, the idea that children explore their parent's personalities is paralleled by the emphasis by Kleinians on the tendency to use concrete metaphors about the infant's wish literally to climb inside and explore the mother's body and to discover all the objects contained inside. According to Aron, patients

> probe their analyst's calm and professional reserve, not only to turn the tables defensively or angrily, but also because people need to connect with others. And they want to connect with others where they live emotionally, where they are authentic and fully present, so they search for information about the other's internal world. [Aron, 1996, p. 80]

Ferenczi (1932) not only anticipated the view that the analyst is pulled into being a participant in the re-enactment of the trauma, he also realized that the patient observes this and reacts to it. As Aron (1996) says, it is not just that the patient misperceives the analyst as being the abuser in the transference but that the patient actually gets the analyst to play that role and then observes the analyst's participation and countertransference responses, and reacts to them. The patient's transference, is, therefore, seen as being not only a distortion but a response to the analyst's countertransference, some of which may be a reflection of the patient, but some that may be more individual to that particular analyst (Sandler, 1993). The patient may therefore be understood to be responding to the repetition—that is, to the therapist's response or countertransference—and this may constitute the failure or the impasse.

Some writers seem to consider that the repetition may not be inevitable—that, as Rosenfeld (1987) suggests, a careful use of technique may avoid these dangers. For example, while Baker (1993) cautions against interventions that could damage a vulnerable patient's self-esteem, confidence, and optimism, he also emphasizes the value of non-interpretive and relationship factors, whereas for Bollas (1987) interpretations are to be played with, not an official decoding. They may be used by the patient in a variety of ways and, as Aron says, can be used as a link with the therapist, played with, loved, clung to, modified, attacked, discarded, transformed, or thrown back. This approach is the notion of two active participants with neither owning the "truth" (Aron, 1996).

Similarly, Levine suggests that "a deeper appreciation of the nature of the analyst's participation in the analytic process and the dimensions of the analytic process to which that participation gives rise may offer us a limited though important safeguard against analytic impasse" (Levine, 1994, p. 675). These "safeguards" are important, of course, although, as has been described earlier, there has been over time a shift of focus from the patient who pushes and prods a neutral analyst to the more object-relations view of the involvement of the analyst in the countertransference, making his own contribution to the repetition. Aron describes this shift in terms of a move away from the traditional model of the neurotic patient who brings irrational childhood wishes, defences, and conflicts into the analysis to be analysed by a relatively mature, healthy, and well-analysed analyst who will study the patient with scientific objectivity and technical neutrality, to one in which the analyst's subjective experience is also to some extent in play in the analytic setting *and* to which the patient is sensitive and responds (Aron, 1996).

While there may be some who see the repetition as avoidable and offer safeguards, it would seem that others consider that the repetition is quite unavoidable, and this is put in very stark terms by Ferenczi:

> I have finally come to realize that it is an unavoidable task of the analyst, although he may behave as he will, he may take kindness and relaxation as far as he possibly can, the time will come when he will have to repeat with his own hands, the act of murder previously perpetrated against the patient. [Ferenczi, 1932, p. 52]

While it may be thought that Ferenczi's views were of his time and extreme, others writing more recently have been preoccupied with similar concerns:

> For my part, I must gradually come to terms with the fact that by my failure to be perfect, I am, in the transference, the traumatising agent and that re-enactment of the traumatising history in its seductive and abandoning aspects is not only likely but inevitable. [Fabricius, 1995, p. 588]

Whether or not this is the case, why, then, should what follows a repetition be a crucial aspect of the trauma, as Balint suggests?

The third phase

The *third phase*, according to Balint, is the real completion of the trauma, although, in the work described in the previous section, the traumatizing aspect of the experience was seen as the part played by the therapist in the repetition—the "countertransference acting out", as Baker describes it (Baker, 1993). As he says, it is the very experience that the patient is driven to repeating, and which he dreads. What, then, of Balint's view that what is traumatic is the failure on the part (in this case) of the therapist to recognize his role? What might contribute to this? What are the possible effects of such failure? And, equally, what might the effect be of such recognition? Understandably, the literature is meagre when it comes to failures, and it may be difficult to own responses like this to one's patients. However, it may be that with the shift to an understanding of the therapeutic relationship in which there are two subjectivities, it is more possible for these ideas to become part of the debate.

Baker (1993) writes about Rosenfeld's willingness to do this with his work. It was Rosenfeld's increasing conviction that many patients had been traumatized in their earlier years and that these environmental traumas had led them to recreate the traumatizing object in the transference. In some of his examples Rosenfeld sees the analyst as having played a crucial part by not recognizing himself as representing the original traumatizing object in the transference. It is noteworthy that Rosenfeld's ideas in this area have not, according to Baker, had the same impact as his earlier unquestionably influential ones. Lack of the acknowledgement of failure may arise out of professional pride, narcissism, or shame—for example, when there is countertransference acting out of hostility or humiliation of the patient. There may be other factors—for example when, as Bollas suggests, the response of the therapist to hearing about a trauma is to be "arrested" by it and not to know what to make of it. Unable to think about it, the therapist needs to recover from the trauma of what he calls "fact presentation". He describes a blank nothing created by the trauma, which interrupts the more fertile exploration of unconscious processes (Bollas, 1995).

This blank nothing may be the patient's response to his traumatic experience as well as the analyst's countertransference to being exposed not only to an account of the experience but also to the patient's dissociated, split-off state. Instead of compassion, there is absence of feeling leading to disbelief in the reality of the experience. This response in the countertransference could be experienced by the patient as a lack of recognition. I am reminded of a patient of mine:

Mr W

Mr W, a young lawyer from Australia, had managed to take care of himself from quite a young age following the breakup of his parents' marriage. He had, without their help, completed his education, come to England, and developed a successful career. He had "never asked for help from anyone"—a caretaker to himself until a relationship with a partner broke down, repeating the breakdown of an earlier relationship and perhaps awakening feelings in him aroused during the end of his parents' marriage. He had been very seriously abused physically by his father during his childhood and adolescence; he had been beaten violently as well as being abused verbally.

My response to the lurid account was a blank, and I found myself wondering whether he was making it up. I felt no sympathy at all for him. His own dissociated state may have communicated itself to me, and I felt little warmth towards him—in fact, I felt quite cut off. He was very punctilious; he did everything with great care and in precise order. His behaviour conveyed a sense of a wish to be extra good. I felt irritated by it and particularly by his increasing tendency to speak in whispers. I began to wish he would go away so I could get on with other patients. Sometimes unspoken thoughts would come to me unbidden: "You're so feeble, you're such a wimp, all you do is moan." I would have a feeling of distancing myself from this rather large adult man talking in a tiny little voice.

It was the emergence in my mind of these rather foreign-sounding words that caused me to consider how I might be experienced by him—that I had become, through projective identification, the abusing father, and that he was protecting himself in the therapy. I continued to keep my distance from him, going through the usual rituals of therapy, making interpretations, yet wishing he would go away. What felt different about this experience was my difficulty of translating my experience into words. I became aware that I was actually afraid of him—afraid that he would attack me and that perhaps his tiny little voice and extra-cautious behaviour were not only to protect him from what I might do to him, but that it served to protect me, in his mind, from what he might do to me.

The potentially traumatizing aspect in this therapy was my rejection of him, going by the name of "therapy" (cf. Ferenczi, 1932). I was distant, disinterested in an emotional sense, yet going through the rituals. At one level, had the patient said something to me indicating that I was being rejecting, I could have pointed his attention to my ongoing concern, as evidenced by my reliability and consistent presence several times a week. Yet it was true, in an emotional sense, and *his* experience of the therapy would have been an accurate one. The real danger would be that this experience of his would be denied by me, because I would refuse to know in an internal sense about my own emotional state.

What was striking for me, on reflection, was my reaction to his account of being abused—a feeling of disbelief, perhaps traumatic for me in the sense that I could not process it. Then there was a sense of being cast in the role of both potential abuser and potential abused, reflected in my inability to elevate the feelings into anything more than feelings and abusive sentences in my mind. Finally, I began slowly to recognize that this irritating and cautious behaviour, though having its beginnings in earlier experiences, was a response to my rejection and negative feelings about him.

None of this was interpreted directly to the patient, though we spoke about anxieties about unpredictability, his and mine, about fears of being rejected, of being dropped. Yet my beginning to acknowledge to myself that not only was there the potential for being perceived as the abuser but that I was responding in a negative and perhaps potentially traumatizing manner brought about a shift in me. I recognized that his irritating behaviour was a response to me (as well as having earlier origins, as mentioned previously) and not only that my distancing and wishing him away was a response to his behaviour.

In relation to Balint's theory, there was the potential—perhaps even actual—traumatization of this patient during the time when I was not able to acknowledge to myself my impact on him. This raises the issue of how the recognition might be conveyed to the patient.

* * *

Since Michael Balint wrote his paper in 1969, there have been considerable advances in technique, which may have gone some way towards preventing the kinds of clear repetitions of re-enactments of the abusing, rejecting parents. Aron points out that Ferenczi anticipated many of these developments and describes aspects of Ferenczi's approach: of acknowledging his own guilt, his description of analysts failing their patients and then honestly acknowledging their mistakes and limitations until the patients and analysts come to mutual forgiveness. All this encompasses the idea of relationships "progressing through sequences of disruption and repair" (Aron, 1996, p. 170).

It was this idea of mutual analysis—the opening of the person of the analyst to the patient—that has been very much questioned by some, although there continues to be a school of thought that considers the idea of self-disclosure to the patient to be therapeutic. Another view is that self-disclosure is more likely to be a burden to the patient and as such potentially invert the relationship, perhaps even be potentially abusive in the sense of primarily fulfilling the needs of the therapist.

The sense in which I have used the word "acknowledgement" is to describe the recognition by the therapist of one's countertransference response to the patient (the repetition) and, in turn, the patient's response to this, which may or may not be verbalized. In the case of Mr W, for example, the understanding that I had of my own reactions to him and their impact on him served as the recognition.

There are other ways—more explicit though not self-disclosing—by which as therapists we can have a negative impact on our patients; for example, what appeared to be a straightforward mistake had the potential for trauma.

Mrs T

Mrs T, a middle-aged woman, waited until towards the end of the session and then explained that what she had to say was extremely difficult, but that she thought I had overcharged her. I asked her what I had charged her and said simply that I was very sorry, I had made a mistake, and I would give her another bill.

I was struck by her tremendous anxiety about broaching the subject with me and wondered with her in the session about it. She said that she had believed that even in the face of evidence, both of us knowing how many sessions she had had, I would continue to insist that I was right and tell her that she did not know what she was talking about. It remained for me to consider for myself why I might have overcharged her. It seemed that she was concerned that I was rejecting of her and that she felt I would make her pay heavily for her need for me. What seemed remarkable to her was that I could acknowledge my mistake and think with her about the meaning. She went on to tell me that her parents had both been very dogmatic and had always insisted on being right, no matter what the issues.

In this instance the patient experienced me initially as the traumatizing object who made mistakes but could never admit them. My capacity to acknowledge, to take in and think about what I had done was a source of amazement to her. The idea that I had a mind that could reflect on my own actions was quite new, perhaps especially in relation to my having made an error.

* * *

In a somewhat different situation, my reaction to a patient's material alarmed her and left her upset and angry.

Mrs S

Mrs S, a married woman in her mid-forties, attractive and charming, returned from a summer break feeling very much restored. Before the break she had been having difficulties with a work colleague, and they had reached an unbearable intensity. She had had similar difficulties in the past and had attempted to keep this from her family because of their overconcern and overinvolvement in her life, which left her feeling that she had no privacy and needed "space" for herself. What had restored her in the break had been the possibility of talking to an aunt with whom she had had a long-standing and reliable relationship. This aunt was connected in some way to a network of therapists and had introduced her to them.

The patient reported being able, for the first time, to express herself to her own family and to these very helpful therapists in a way that she felt truly reflected her own feelings. As she spoke, I began to feel more and more demeaned by her account. I thought of all the years of work with her, now somehow rubbished, when I had actually thought that we had both struggled through some difficult times and reached some understanding. I felt the narcissistic blow, my professional talents impugned, and said, "You felt that what I had to offer was not enough?" Usually amenable, her anger flared, and she said she thought there was something very healthy about being able to talk to a lot of people. She left the session angry and miserable after having arrived at her session feeling so much better.

When she came for her session the following day, she was withdrawn and resentful. In the interim I had considered my intervention, what I had felt that had prompted it, and what it might have meant to her. I knew that she was terrified of being openly angry with me. As she usually spoke easily but was now in a silent fury, I said that I thought she was angry with me because of my comment yesterday and that perhaps I had conveyed to her a sense that I wanted her exclusively for myself, that she should not have significant relationships with others. She began talking about the exclusivity that she felt had been the characteristic of her relationship with her mother. She said that she had come to the session feeling furious with me, but now that had gone. Perhaps, she said, it was because of being able to talk about it. I said perhaps it was that but also the feeling of relief that I might have a mind that could reflect not only on what she brought to the session but on what I brought as well.

* * *

There was no self-disclosure or mutual analysis in the usual meaning of these phrases. *What seemed to be important was the recognition of the patient's response to my countertransference.* What would have completed the trauma, in Balint's terms, would have been to have denied the validity of her response—for example, by my denying that I had reacted angrily to Mrs S. I might have pursued that interpretation, saying that all I had said was that "You felt that what I had to offer was not enough." I could have linked it to thoughts that, during the break, I had been unfaithful to her, and so she was retaliating by doing the same to me. The effect of that would then have been my denial of my response. This could have led to the kind of arrest described by Bollas (1993) and comparable to what Fonagy (Fonagy, Moran, Edgcumbe, Kennedy, &

Target, 1993) refers to as "inhibited mental processes". Bollas describes the children of parents who are impinging and acutely traumatizing, where the effect is of preventing symbolic elaboration. The traumatized person will behave in a way that controls psychic damage, preventing the self from being exposed to further psychic damage. Rosenfeld describes this in terms of a sense of profound isolation:

> As I see it, one of the most important facts which had to be considered about the traumatic experience is that the patient has had to cope all on his own sometimes for a considerable time. Often he has survived only through such severe reactions as denial, splitting and depersonalisation. [Rosenfeld, 1987, p. 36]

Perhaps the completion of the trauma can be seen as *emotional exile:* the person who had been trusted has responded in a way that has caused pain, humiliation, or anger. At such a time it would be that person—the therapist—to whom the patient would turn for understanding or comfort. By not being available, like the exile, there is no return, the link has been severed, the object has been destroyed.

Both Bollas and Fonagy consider how the process of arrest or inhibition can be unlocked. According to Bollas, the children of parents who are "generative" develop through the successful elaboration of idiom, and will develop an open-mindedness to the contributing effects of the object world—an openness that those who are traumatized may in a self-protective way seek to avoid. The following quotation about how this may be undone in the analysis gives the sense of the importance of the recognition by the analyst of his contribution to what has gone wrong:

> Our errors of association, corrected by the analysand—or "destroyed" through a use-change of them—assist in the ordinary essential deconstruction of analytical certainty. If we impose our models of the mind upon the patient, as we cannot fail to do, let us equally bare a shared witness to the reliable deconstruction of such authority. Therein, lies a potential balance, between the necessary ambition that authorises our search to find the truth and the ineffable movement of uncon-

scious processes that keeps us as democratic representatives in the assembly of consciousness rather than monarchs of an imposed truth. [Bollas, 1993, pp. 132–133]

Implicit in this quotation is the on-going process of self-reflection in the analyst, which Bollas perhaps puts explicitly in an earlier work: "in order to find the patient we must look for him within ourselves" (Bollas, 1987).

Fonagy's work focuses more on the intersubjective nature of the experience, exploring how the reflective capacity may be acquired through an intersubjective process, such that the child's growing recognition of the importance of mental states (feelings, beliefs, desires, and intentions) arises through the shared understanding of his own mental world and that of his caregiver. He suggests that with patients with inhibited mental processes, interpretations remain crucial to reactivating these processes. They offer the possibility of presenting alternative views of mental events but, more importantly, involve the analyst in becoming actively involved in the mental functioning of the patient and create the possibility of the patient becoming reciprocally involved with the working of the analyst's mind. The experience of mental involvement with another human being without the threat of overwhelming mental anguish he sees as being vital to the process. The therapist who cannot acknowledge his role in a traumatic experience has, in a sense, the last word on the subject—the dialogue is over. In contrast, the therapist who can acknowledge his role continues the dialogue.

With Mrs S, I carried the experience of anger and continued to think about and analyse my own feelings. I realized that she was affected by it and acknowledged this by linking it to my comment. There was an on-going dialogue instead of the emotional exile; the link had been maintained. There had been survival, and it was not only survival of the therapist but survival of the therapeutic process, an on-going process that Baker refers to as the new object— "the process that perceives, facilitates, remembers, anticipates and gratifies the patient's needs" (Baker, 1993). Does such a process require that the patient becomes involved with the mental state of the therapist, as Fonagy suggests, without the threat of overwhelming mental anguish? Recognition then may convey to the patient that there has been this kind of survival, the dialogue has not ended.

* * *

I have tried in this chapter to take Balint's views on trauma forward, partly because he considered the views of Freud to be incomplete. He had not been able to develop his ideas but had hoped that there would be fruitful development by others. Perhaps in some ways his ideas were ahead of his time and for them to be developed in a clinical context required all the advances in thinking that there have been in the field of countertransference: the shift from the countertransference as a source of information about the patient's unconscious to the idea of the countertransference reflecting aspects of the therapist's own unconscious and subjective experience. A further development was the idea that the patient's transference may be not only a distorted response but a response to the therapist's countertransference. These developments made it possible to consider Balint's central premise—that the completion of the trauma is the failure on the part of the object to recognize his role in it. Both a failure of recognition and the recognition of the role were considered.

The traumatizing object that has no capacity to recognize and reflect on itself has been destroyed and can, therefore, no longer be the source of love and care and attention. In contrast, the traumatizing object that has the capacity to reflect on itself, and on itself in relation to the other, remains a source of love and care and attention: the very act of recognition is an expression of this. It suggests the existence of a mind with a potential for further reflections and for a continuing dialogue with itself and the other. It is a mind that has survived and that facilitates what Winnicott, when writing about the mother–infant relationship, refers to as "going on being" (Winnicott, 1960d, 1962). Perhaps Bion shared Balint's view when he said:

> One may deplore an unfortunate decision; how terrible it might be if we never made unfortunate decisions or unfortunate interpretations. In analysis it is recovery from the unfortunate decision, the use of the mistaken decision that we have to accustom ourselves to deal with. [Bion, 1977, p. 50]

point that there has been no kind of change of the dimension in the block.

CHAPTER SEVEN

Erotic transference and its vicissitudes in the countertransference

Viqui Rosenberg

> I am in love's wrong place, which is its dazzling place. The darkest place, according to a Chinese proverb, is always underneath the lamp.
>
> [Roland Barthes, 1977]

The relative scarcity of writing on the erotic transference and the obstacles posed in my own mind when I set out to explore this theme may not be unrelated. Already in 1915, Freud says that it is this form of transference that "held back the development of psychoanalytic therapy during the first decade" (Freud, 1915a). Heeding this well-worn warning, I prepare for the task while still preoccupied by these questions:

(a) How will I deal with confidentiality regarding clinical examples?
(b) What will my colleagues think about me when they read this?
(c) Is it really true that the patients who now come to mind seem all to be linked to the profession in one way or another?

Turning to the literature on the subject, I look for reassurance and instruction in the ways that other writers have dealt with these concerns. There is a range of strategies to be found there. It is possible to keep a narrow focus on patient and pathology, to discuss perversions and psychotic enactments as well as infantile longings and resistance, to focus on working alliances and attachments, always locating the stage largely in the patient's emotional life. There is a marked tendency for the therapist to remain anonymous, because this is in the nature of professional presentations and, in any case, the analytic process strives to uncover the unconscious world of our patients with as little interference as possible from our own.

However, it is well known that love matters are written on a special page. The intimacy and exclusiveness and passion of this emotion constitute a natural attack on neutrality; this two-person event cannot but "threaten the tranquillity of the therapist" (Bergmann, 1994).

In a recent article entitled "Is the Transference Feared by the Psychoanalyst?", Grinberg writes: "After all, even those analysts who proclaim the importance of the transference and characterize themselves as making predominantly "transference interpretations" often do not dare to penetrate the deepest and most regressive levels of the transference because they unconsciously fear that this might commit their emotions excessively" (Grinberg, 1997, p. 5). It may be this fear that creates a relative vacuum in the literature as well as the potential for a vacuum in the thinking that erotic transference eventually demands of the practitioner.

I shall now go back to those uneasy questions of mine and attempt to shift their "obstacle" status by turning them into starting points to my discussion. I shall do this because I suspect that the questions themselves are formulations in disguise. As psychotherapy offers an opportunity for the reworking of parent–child dependency issues, it follows that its erotic components will carry the illicit quality characteristic of incestuous feelings. Perhaps my initial questions offer the potential to elucidate some significant countertransferential aspects that arise in the presence of the erotic transference.

Confidentiality, exposure, and identification

To write about the erotic elements that are a necessary component of transference elicits a feeling of danger and exposure; there is a contradiction implied in making public such private, fragile, and yet legitimate aspects of the therapeutic project. Uncovering such intimate feelings proposes itself as an illicit pursuit that carries a sense of betrayal—betrayal of the patient's trusting feelings, betrayal of the therapeutic ideals of neutrality, betrayal of our own loved ones. . . .

Love is one of the most actual and concrete emotions to be found in the transference: in the presence of love, to continue implacably with the analytic work of interpretation feels to be denying or diminishing its truthfulness and actuality. Its often fragile and impermanent nature can be easily unmasked, depriving the patient of a full transitional experience where the therapist can—in the Winnicottian sense—be invented and destroyed. It is therefore necessary to tolerate and to contain the emotional charge of the situation and also to exercise a great deal of caution in order to avoid the therapist's own defensive use of premature interpretation at a moment in which the relationship threatens "to commit [one's] emotions excessively" (Grinberg, 1997).

And yet, at which point does the uninterpreted erotic transference become an uncomfortably shared secret? Inhibitions against recognizing and fully including erotic elements in clinical accounts may mirror similar difficulties in the analytic encounter. These uninterpreted elements can fester like a perverse collusion, a sado-masochistic enactment that engulfs psychotherapist and patient in a paralysing unspoken pact.

To say or not to say poses a crucial question within the treatment, usually experienced at two different levels: (a) Which is the appropriate timing to formulate an interpretation?; (b) At which level should the interpretation be addressed—that is, adult sexuality or infantile attachment?

Some of the questions posed here may account for the infrequency with which erotic transference fully enters the fabric of clinical expositions; its discussion tends to be left for the purpose-built papers that pay attention to the erotic in its most reified forms—for example, breakdown of treatment, perversions, psychosis. "Both reverence and bias contribute(d) to the failure of thinking about the erotic transference to keep pace with the rest of psychoanalytic development" (Hill, 1994, p. 488).

Confidentiality already has an awkward place in the field of psychoanalytic literature. While it would be clearly impoverishing to do altogether without illustrations, it is not easy to find a sound reason why a practitioner should erupt into the inner world of a former or current patient in order to request permission to write their own account of what happened in the therapy.

But, however complex this issue is already, it increases in complexity at the prospect of presenting clinical material that illustrates the erotic transference to professional colleagues. The therapist's preoccupations may inadvertently denote the narcissistic elements that are easily brought into play by erotic transference and its vicissitudes in the countertransference. The material may be perceived as a crass attempt to display the therapist's "irresistible charms" (Freud, 1915a) and refer the reader straight to the writer's exhibitionistic tendencies.

Indeed, there are certain clinical accounts, often *a propos* some other matters, that seem to place the reader in the role of voyeuristic outsider or else sceptical critic; the vignette may not have been designed to illustrate what it actually does when perceived from outside as a display of the therapist's love for their creation and an idealization of the patient and/or the therapy, which threatens to impregnate the narrative and render it void in respect of its original intention. When this phenomenon prevails, it can be said that the patient has been narcissistically cathected in a manner that Searles aptly describes as: "the appeal which the gratifyingly improving patient makes to the narcissistic residue in the analyst's personality, the Pygmalion in him" (Searles, 1959, p. 187). That is to say, we have encountered one of the sources from which countertransferential oedipal love flows, and although this may well be a benign unconscious response to our patients' need to be accepted and appreciated, it still causes embarrassment to be seen doing something that one had not intended to show—surely another good reason to keep at a good distance from areas that are likely to expose the therapist's unconscious.

It is a requirement of love that lovers should have some capacity for mutual identification. In the therapeutic relationship, it is also required from therapist and patient to be open to lovingly identifying with one another for the purposes of communication and understanding. This way the scene is set for the exercise of loving capacities that are an essential part of the psychoanalytic process. However, it is this very requirement that in turn creates paths for more primitive erotic urges to claim a way of expression and communication. Erotic and sexual transferences can take hold, with their idiosyncratic ways of acting both as a vehicle as well as an obstacle to the therapeutic enterprise.

But although the erotic transference can constitute itself as a powerful form of resistance, it is also true that there are many patients who, while sustaining relatively strong erotic feelings towards the therapist, do not seem to destroy the treatment. It is, rather, the case that the erotic component of the identification becomes largely sublimated in a variety of ways. The therapist may enjoy the talents of the patient and his or her achievements; the patient "does well" in the treatment and in other areas of life; both parties reap the benefit of a certain complicity that has erotic traces but remains in check as a creative force. Of course, there are potentially less happy evolutions where narcissistic complicity may grip therapist and patient into mutual idealization, and this dynamic, which allows no room for failure or mourning if it becomes fixed, is one of the various routes leading to therapeutic impasse.

Another path to the resolution of intense erotic feelings lies in the patient's attempt to internalize the therapist by acquiring their best perceived identity. A form of sublimation is found by transforming the desire to possess the loved object into the will to become like it. And thus the patient becomes a psychotherapist. Whether the phantasy results in a life project or remains a metaphor, the opportunity arises again to mourn the real losses that it entails. It is perhaps even more remarkable when, as a result of the demand that the aspiring psychotherapist should go into a training analysis, the original (loved) therapist has to be given up. It is appropriate that these patients should find themselves in a second analysis where hopefully there will be a renewed opportunity to work through the remnants of previously unresolved erotic transferences.

The question remains as to what extent these unanalysed transferences—whether to the first or the second therapist—are responsible for some of the ways in which members of our profession cathect psychoanalysis. Incestuous idealization and hierarchic rigidity constitute possible distortions of unresolved primitive erotic strivings where one idea or institution comes to represent the idealized lost object.

As is evident from these introductory remarks, the nature of the subject requires that it should be explored by placing apprehension underneath the lamp and accepting that this is indeed the type of transference that evokes the strongest and most varied feelings in the therapist. Erotic transference becomes a difficult topic because it always implies a countertransferential ordeal. In the presence of our patients' love we experience warmth, excitement, alarm, disgust, fear, entrapment, complicity, guilt, irritation, and so many other emotions that call for self-scrutiny and for the capacity for containment.

A new set of questions now arises: Is the erotic transference "loving"? And is the patient's love the same as the therapist's love? The 1991 *Shorter Oxford English Dictionary on Historical Principles* entry for "love" reads: "That state of feeling with regards to a person which arises from recognition of attractive qualities, from sympathy, or from natural ties, and manifests itself in warm affection and attachment." This definition suggests three main areas of reference: recognition of attractive qualities, sympathy, the idea of natural ties.

At least at the start of a treatment, it could be said that patients have little opportunity to recognize attractive qualities in their therapists except for what can hopefully be experienced as a "listening" quality. Meanwhile, it is the therapist's task to embark on a detailed discovery of the patient's qualities, attractive and otherwise, and it is normally expected that this process will engender "sympathy" in both parties. Indeed, genuine love will eventually be called for in order to take the endeavour to a satisfactory conclusion; but to begin with, the situation requires that the therapist should exercise loving capacities in a more active way than the patient consciously will.

However, it is the idea of natural ties that exercises the patient. After all, the therapeutic frame is there to elicit the memory of the original familial world and its attachments, and this must be the source from which the patient's love for the therapist flows, based on the phantasy of natural ties.

The blend of the patient's phantasy and the therapist's labour contributes to the intensity of the emotion, and under certain circumstances it can fuse in a transferential situation that seems to fall beyond the realms of interpretation.

Seeking clinical material for what I wish to describe, I am struck by my reluctance to bring in illustrations of extreme pathology. I believe that to give cases of, for example, perverse sexualization permits a differentiation between the feelings of the patient and those of the therapist that would not enlighten this particular discussion. What I am trying to explore here is the territory in which the erotic transference is not easily liable to idealization or denigration, or can be clearly defined as only belonging to "the other". It is the sort of everyday clinical occurrence that confronts therapists with their own ordinary responses, embarrassed and clumsy, where sometimes feelings of desire and hate alternate with revealing insights. These are painful moments in a treatment where confusion and the blurring of boundaries disorganize the therapist's thinking capacities. It does indeed feel like "the wrong place", next to the dazzling light of the lamp, utterly visible and yet blinded by the strength of our own emotions.

Erotic, eroticized, sexualized transferences

Freud and many authors after him have helpfully established distinctions within the broad spectrum of transference-love manifestations. Both in "The Dynamics of Transference" (1912b) and in "Observations on Transference-love" (1915a), Freud remarks on the paradox by which this form of transference is hijacked by resistance and yet also reveals the potential for discovering the nature of the patient's most primitive object, thus offering the opportunity for "bringing all that is most deeply hidden in the patient's erotic life into her consciousness and therefore under her control" (1915a). He does, however, famously warn us against a special category (of women) not amenable to analysis who are "accessible only to the logic of soup, with dumplings for arguments"—a rather unfortunate metaphor for those patients whom today we would describe as not sufficiently "psychologically minded".

Rappaport (1956), Blum (1994), Bolognini (1994), and others elaborate on these distinctions and establish several categories along the spectrum of transference-love, ranging from affection to perverse hostility. For the purpose of this exposition I will circumscribe these manifestations to three distinctive levels: *erotic*, *eroticized*, and *sexualized* transference.

The *erotic* end of the spectrum evokes the parent/child relationship, and, in spite of its emotional intensity, it is capable of recognizing the "as if" element that can eventually be referred back to the internal world of the patient. The *eroticized* transference belongs with borderline manifestations where the therapist is idealized as well as found to be persecuting. It denotes the patient's limitations within the symbolic realm and results in a powerful actualization of concrete and primitive passions, while, in as much as it is hijacked by resistance, it is accompanied by the patient's loss of purpose in respect of the original therapeutic aim. The *sexualized* transference largely describes the hostile and destructive use of erotization to attack the treatment as well as the therapist, as usually manifested in the perversions.

Although most psychotherapists would be able to find in their practices relatively pure examples of the *sexualized* transference, psychotherapeutic work moves largely in a realm where neither of the two other categories exists exclusively or can be attributed singly to a specific patient and their treatment. The *erotic* and the *eroticized* often alternate in the course of one single therapy; in its extreme, the *eroticized* transference is of course the most primitive and threatening, sometimes giving way to intense sexualization, occasionally becoming a violent instrument of resistance and resulting, to the relief of the therapist, in a premature ending.

More frequently, erotic transference is threaded into the fabric of the therapy, making special and more disturbing appearances in dreams or fantasies, at times enhanced by alterations to the frame such as holiday breaks or accidental meetings with other patients who help to reactivate the oedipal conflict. If the superego is not overwhelming, it is possible for the patient to disclose and explore these love pangs as well as the accompanying feelings of jealousy and exclusion, and thus eventually to become aware of the therapist's genuine interest and acceptance. Indeed, this very experience reinforces the sense that psychotherapy offers a special intimacy that can be confused with eroticism but that, in fact, has its own distinctive uniqueness worth preserving and treasuring. This type of occurrence is more akin to oedipal love on its way to resolution, where the erotic urges can be renounced in order to protect the integrity of the loved objects.

When erotic feelings are unacceptable to the superego, they must be kept within the limbo of repression. It is possible for erotic transference to be concealed with iron determination, which results in highly stilted verbal communications often character-ized by prolonged, stifling silences. There are, of course, other reasons why silence takes hold of a therapy, and it takes time for the practitioner to discern the colouring of this particular form of absence. The silence itself, as well as the paucity or irrelevance of what is actually said, can fill the therapist with impatience, despondency, or dread. None of these countertransferential re-sponses contributes to the state of mind to be relied upon in order to make useful interpretations; the therapist feels caught in a cob-web where thinking has slowed down and there is no sense of perspective from which to get a fuller view.

A young male patient comes to mind, whose defences illus-trate this configuration. He referred himself hoping to be helped with depressive episodes, which he consciously linked to work pressure. During a long initial period he presented a narrow discourse confined to professional matters; if there was a break in work, he felt as if there was nothing to report, and he became anxious and negative about attending sessions. The hostile and deadening depression did not shift: on the con-trary, he successfully projected his feelings into me and left me struggling to emerge from a sense of numbness and resent-ment at the end of each session. However, I did gradually be-come aware that this man waited to be fetched from the waiting-room in his own idiosyncratic way: I heard him re-peatedly wipe his feet on the mat, as if he were marking his territory, and as I opened the door to let him in he would be standing, fully facing me, in a way that I found somewhat intimidating. The rest was meek awkwardness and silence.

It is a matter of serious consideration how to interpret behaviour that takes place at the edges of the session. To comment on it carries the high risk of pushing underground what was meant to be brought to the surface—that is, the unconscious meaning of what is being enacted. In the present case, to interpret this particular ritual as a form of sexualization would either have panicked the patient or been experienced by him as a seduction. On the other hand, to leave this fragment of interaction on the other side of the door was equivalent to leaving out the most alive and spontaneous manifestation that this patient brought to therapy. Further work had to take place in order to create a ripeness that would allow an acknowledgement of the erotic in the session. Interpretations were aimed at uncovering the patient's anger, which underpinned his work difficulties and the attachment as well as hostility that he felt towards the therapist, the need to conceal which lay beneath his silences. The patient was eventually able to recall several dreams about himself and the therapist: either a bed or the couch featured largely with them as husband and wife involved in a sexless affair: sitting in bed, reading. It still continued to be hard to tell at which point unconscious censorship became conscious concealment, but the long silences always seemed to signal a "no-go" area. Although the periods of acute depression continued, it became possible to agree that they should be more accurately described as "attacks of repression" on his aggressive and sexual impulses. When these impulses were in the ascendant, he drained the life out of them—as he did in sessions—by metaphorically curling up in a ball and becoming listless, cut off, and exhausted with tension.

The dilemma at this point in the therapy had been to find how to loosen the grip of the repression without blowing it apart and risking an unmanageable crisis. Even after the appearance of the dreams, it did not feel possible to interpret the erotic transference at a genital level but only as infantile attachment and a child-like phantasy of marrying mother. However incomplete, this level of interpretation already represented an important opening in the patient's capacity to understand symbolic meaning; it paved the way towards acknowledgement of the repressed eroticized transference, which—when named—could stand a better chance of promotion to an erotic "as if" transference. It was only from this position that this patient's love and desire for the therapist could be accepted and integrated as a lively component of his character. As the erotic wishes were increasingly acknowledged in the transference, they became, at the same time, introduced into the symbolic realm.

Ms X

The following clinical material illustrates a different defensive configuration, where the patient appeared to have lost all interest in the original aim of therapy and overwhelmed the sessions with her erotic concerns. Her discourse was tense and stilted, characterized by the absence of themes such as health, sex, or any ailments that could consciously place her body at the centre of my attention. She did, however, speak frequently about clothes and make-up, while, as she later acknowledged, she quietly despaired at my lack of comment regarding her well-groomed appearance. This patient eventually acknowledged that she dressed up carefully for each session, hoping to arouse my sexual interest, but—while the preoccupation that something sexual should happen was predominant in her mind—she had no intention of bringing her sexuality for analysis. I was gradually alerted to these enactments and became very conscious of the patient's sexual display, and yet felt that there was no way of referring to this that would not be experienced either as accepting her sexual invitation or, alternatively, as a humiliating "dressing-down" of the patient's fantasies. The obvious alternative—to interpret this behaviour as the patient's infantile wish to become special to mother—was met with anger and irritation. She did not wish anything analytic to upset the romantic prospect. Her otherwise agile mind was almost exclusively engaged in avoiding therapy and in watching carefully for any clues that might help her in accomplishing her new aim: to make her therapist fall in love with her. When this aspect of the therapy became a central force, I felt quite redundant; communication was cautious on both sides, and the patient had little availability to her own associations. For different reasons, both our energies were largely invested in censoring the erotic: the patient wanted the erotic to be enacted rather than analysed, while I wanted to make certain that I would not unconsciously gratify this wish.

This patient dreamt repeatedly that she visited her therapist socially and that, in one or another way, she made a mess on her carpet, which she then tried to clear up. This dream expressed the anxiety she felt at the possibility of spilling her secret contents in the consulting-room, the therapist representing an internal unaccepting mother who could only love her as a sexualized, narcissistic extension of herself. Although she unconsciously wished for the therapist/mother to receive her infantile messy contents, she felt driven to get her acceptance by becoming the therapist's object of erotic desire.

There were other enactments in the treatment—mainly around time-keeping and seeking to satisfy her curiosity—which were often strikingly concrete and difficult to integrate and to process, consistent with the type of defensive mechanisms employed by the erotization of transference. All this material furnished the therapy with a vivid experience of the emotional elements that had been unbearable to the patient in her early life. Through projective identification, my own feelings were enlisted to register the impact of this patient's psychic distress.

Both these treatments aroused strong feelings in the countertransference as well as the anxiety that the untimely interpretation of the erotic transference could become an act of self-defence, driven by the need to dilute acutely uncomfortable situations. In both of these cases I experienced myself right "in the thick of it", at times enduring the densely loaded atmosphere of the session and at other times taking the position of a detached and often irritable participant.

Ardent human feelings that are not corresponded are distressing to witness and can trigger an urge to seek refuge in denial or alienation, all of which induces an array of emotions in the therapist that require elucidation. Some of these emotions may be projected by the patient, and some constitute the therapist's own

response to the demands of the situation, as well as her own transference to the patient and the circumstances. Racker says: "in
countertransference various aspects of the Oedipal situation are
repeated. . . . Although the neurotic reactions of countertransference may be sporadic, the predisposition to them is continuous"
(Racker, 1968).

Thus the therapist's changing capacities to recognize her/his
own transference to the patient and the situation play their role
and have a significant influence on the fluctuation between the
erotic and the eroticized as it unfolds in the treatment.

The emotional density that often signals the presence of unconscious erotic strivings is illustrated by the following vignette:

In the first session of the week—the last week before a holiday—Ms X seems to have overcome her deep apprehension
about the break. Everything has fallen into place, she explains.
She gives a day-by-day and week-by-week account of her future plans and adds that she now feels pleasantly busy and
spoken for until the end of the holiday. I too feel relieved, since
this patient has been very distressed in the recent past, and I
have had my own concerns about leaving her to manage on
her own. Towards the end of the session I interpret that she
must be relieved to be able to give such a detailed account of
her activities for the break and that to do so makes her feel that
I will now be able to carry her in my mind and think of her
every day. The patient becomes silent for a while, and I sit
contentedly, thinking of what has been achieved during the
past few months, as well as perhaps anticipating the pleasures
of my imminent holiday. Time catches up with me, and I an-
nounce the end of the session. It is only then that I realize that
my patient has been quietly crying. As she rises from the
couch, she murmurs in a rather menacing tone something
about my bad timing.

The next day Ms X says on arrival that "it is a miracle" that she
is here on time; the underground has come to a halt, and while
she was finding alternative routes she had worried about what
I would think if she were late. There are clearly various twists
to this statement, but I can at least infer that she does not wish
me to think that she wanted to be late. What slowly unravels in

the course of the session is that she found my interpretation of the previous day deeply humiliating. It seemed to her that her erotic feelings for me had been found out and deemed inappropriate. In addition—and as it could be expected—I had then triumphantly turned her out of the room. Her anger at my rejection and her wish to retaliate by not coming back could only be further proof of the inappropriateness of her feelings and would be better kept secret. However, although she could have arrived late, she did not and, moreover, she now tells me what she had sought to conceal!

For my part, I have a heavy heart about my bad timing of the previous day. Surely I had tried to forget the remains of her previous distress; and how could I not notice that she was crying? And, in any case, why did I wait so long to make the interpretation? Is it possible that I did not notice that Ms X was crying because unconsciously I wished to deny the implications of it, resenting my patient's "bad timing", so close to the coming break; so much wanting for myself a "good ending" that would allow me a carefree departure? And to what extent could I have been trying to turn a blind eye to her erotic feelings, thus confirming my patient's idea that they should better be kept outside the therapy? Of course, all these thoughts are rushing to my mind alongside the patient's angry tears.

I can say now that some of my self-recriminations are technically appropriate and that some lead directly to the nature of this patient's persecutory internal objects and that, in addition, some others would have been triggered by my own guilty feelings.

I think that the turmoil of concurrent emotions described above is rather characteristic of the way in which the erotic transference sets the scene. Both the patient and the therapist find themselves *underneath the lamp*—that is, in the darkest place. They are indeed visible from outside while they themselves are blinded by the brilliance of the heat. Intense emotions in the patient and the therapist pour into the same mould, to gel together and create a rather impenetrable fabric. It is true that the variations of transference-love, ranging from sexualized to highly symbolic, evoke different responses in the countertransference, but the fact remains that all those responses carry a strong and intimate component for the therapist. On this matter, Hill comments: "Freud recommends that analysts, like Odysseus, chain themselves to the psychoanalytic mast of transference analysis in order to tolerate the ordeal of listening to their own and their patients' Sirens" (Hill, 1994, p. 485). The emotions that arise in the course of a psychotherapy always contain the potential to merge with both parties' infantile longings and thus elicit a re-enactment of primitive dynamics.

Sublimation and its vicissitudes

These clinical fragments have in common the fact that the erotic presented itself at a relatively early stage of the treatment and that the patients did not—in any consistent way—elicit transferences in the therapist that could have added her own erotic strivings to theirs. It is of course not always the case that a therapy is comparatively free from the therapist's own feelings of attraction and desire. If not from the outset, it is an eventual necessity that in due course patients will engage their therapist's loving emotions. Searles talks movingly and perceptively about the oedipal transference that reproduces the parent's love and desire for the child and requires "the analyst's deeply-felt relinquishment of the patient both as being a cherished infant, and as being a fellow adult who is responded to at the level of genital love" (Searles, 1959, p. 181). It is at this point that the work of mourning in the oedipal transference becomes hardest and most painful, both because the therapist is confronted with one of the mysteries of their occupational choice—that of having to love and to lose—and because it is also possible for the patient to perceive, at least unconsciously, that they have indeed become special.

The wish to reach a compromise can take a particularly intractable form of collusive defence, since both patient and therapist are united in their motivation to achieve a less painful outcome. Although there is great variety of ways in which the therapeutic couple embarks on the painstaking elaboration of mourning and ending, I believe that in some cases this work falls short of completion by taking the form of a pseudo-resolution imposed by the patient's decision to become a psychotherapist. Since the capacity to tolerate imperfection is an integral part of analytic practice, this "good-enough" solution to some of the dilemmas presented by the erotic transference needs not to be judged as unsatisfactory. It is, after all, a sublimation and therefore an important achievement in the therapy. It is only in the measure in which it is not perceived in its limitations that it erodes the sound foundations of our profession. Should we become practitioners, then if we have not had a thorough chance to examine our oedipal transferences, we will not, of course, be very useful to our patients, but equally we become liable to unduly idealize psychoanalysis and its institutions. The infantile strivings that remained unconscious during psychotherapy, merged with the therapist's own limitations in this respect, can all find an opportunity to address themselves to what seems to present itself as a safer object or as an objective truth: psychoanalysis. It was precisely on the questions of religion and nationalism, in his paper on *Group Psychology and the Analysis of the Ego* that Freud (1921c) brilliantly described identification in its primitive orality as a form of regression from object-choice. He talks about the overvaluation of the object of sexual desire and the role of repression in the transformation of this object by putting it in the place of the ego ideal and remarks:

> It is interesting to see that it is precisely *those sexual impulsions that are inhibited in their aims* which achieve such lasting ties between people. . . . It is the fate of sensual love to become extinguished when it is satisfied; for it to be able to last, it must from the beginning be mixed with purely affectionate components—with such, that is, as are inhibited in their aims—or it must itself undergo a transformation of this kind. [Freud, 1921c, p. 115]

It is of the essence of the psychoanalytic process that transference-love in its erotic form should "*undergo a transformation*". In any of its manifestations—be it compliance, hostility, seduction, identification—it will always require that patient and therapist should go through the labours of maturation and mourning; and it is the therapist who must remain alert to the many vicissitudes on this path. There seem to be few other instances in our profession where our passions and those of our patients have such potential for fusion and confusion. And just when at their most subtle and sophisticated, erotic feelings can in fact present us with their most challenging defensive constructions. What appears as a successful therapeutic outcome can mask a natural reluctance to experience mourning and loss, which finds a reprieve in the patient's act of embracing the psychoanalytic profession and offers therapist and patient the illusion of not having to give up their oedipal romance. It is here that analysis can illuminate the darkest corners of primitive phantasy. Of course, the outcome is not prescriptive. All choices are, after all, over-determined, and that of a professional vocation such as this has to be fuelled by passion in order to see us through the dedication that it demands.

But the fact remains that we need to understand this choice in its limitations as well as in its scope. To become a psychoanalytic practitioner does not represent a triumph against separation and uncertainty but, rather, an acceptance of our limited capacities to endure painful reality, as well as the opportunity to re-work these issues again and again. That this opportunity—and its pitfalls— should lie hidden beneath our very front doorstep constitutes yet another paradox in the rich world of psychoanalysis.

CHAPTER EIGHT

Dreaming and day-dreaming

Anna Witham

> "A dream is a private work of art. Like all art it is, in Picasso's
> phrase, a fiction that brings us nearer reality."
>
> [Klauber, 1986]

A dream comes from sources in the mind that are the fun-
damentals of our individuality. These sources are located
in the unconscious. Interpreting and understanding reported dreams can bring us closer to the wellsprings of our unconscious life and the truthful reality and mine of memory that it
contains. Conversely, it is part of psychoanalytical thinking that
conscious fantasy, the day-dream, can take the mind away from
the creative rigour of the internal world's processes and lead it, at
worst, into a stultifying nowhere. Freud's view was that dreams
and day-dreams were structured by the same internal psychic
processes, and the dream-work was essentially the same, based on
displacement, symbolization, condensation, and secondary revision. It is, of course, the latter that has an especially important
function in day-dreaming. So we have the intriguing paradox that

151

dreams and day-dreams are the same and yet are essentially different—a paradox that suits the dreaming world and the mind of the dreamer.

I begin my exploration by considering dreams and their relationship to creativity, and I go on to look at the context of dreams—namely, sleep—and consider what states of mind there might be, other than being asleep or being awake. I then discuss the ways in which conscious fantasy and day-dreams may be the same and may be different.

The dream

Freud's own creativity was clearly manifest in *The Interpretation of Dreams* (Freud, 1900a). There he laid down the scholarly basis for his recognition of the importance of dreams and dreaming for clinical psychoanalysis. This, in turn, was part of the development of the topographical model of the mind, where the structured revelation of the unconscious (*UCs*) via the guardianship of the conscious (*Cs*) and pre-conscious (*PCs*), could be witnessed. Since 1900, the dream has remained the classic, illustrative evidence in clinical psychoanalysis of the manifestation and workings of the unconscious, in spite of the fact that the focus on dreams and their interpretation in the consulting-room has undergone many vicissitudes over the century of psychoanalytic work. An early indication of the demise of the dream as a central focus can be seen in the fact that for the first 12 years of its publication, the *International Journal of Psychoanalysis* devoted an entire section to the analysis of patients' dreams, but in 1932 this section was dropped (Flanders, 1993). When Freud reviewed his thinking on dreams in *The New Introductory Lectures* (1933a, Lecture XXIX), he did not endeavour to change the theoretical basis of the topographical model, of the *Cs*, the *UCs*, and the *PCs*, to that of the newer structural theory of id, ego, and superego, which had been developed in 1923, some nine years earlier (Freud, 1923b).

Freud always saw "the Dream book", as he referred to it, as his greatest achievement: "Insight such as this falls to one's lot but once a lifetime" (Freud, 1932e [1931]). The forcefulness in the original work has sustained it as a body of knowledge and a text of note in psychoanalysis, despite the fact that continuing developments in psychoanalytic thinking and theorizing have, for many people, long left behind its theoretical basis. There have, of course, been attempts to bring Freud's ideas on dreams within the purview of the later structural theory. Brenner's paper (1969) is one such attempt. His argument is that dream analysis is no longer so uniquely important as a method of understanding unconscious processes. He suggests that free association, jokes, daydreams, responses to culture, character traits, sexual practices, and preferences are all responses to the interplay between the internal forces of id, ego, and superego.

However, this attempt to dissolve the significance of the dream does not quite fit with clinical experience. When a patient brings a dream, the psychoanalytic psychotherapist knows that the work has engaged the unconscious. This may be a confirming experience for the therapist and for the patient. Sometimes, when a dream is reported towards the end of a session, it can be understood as a confirmation of the work that has already been done in the previous 50 minutes (Limentani: personal communication). However, one must concur that the evolution and increasing sophistication of clinical psychoanalysis in focusing on the transferential culture of the session has meant that there is less reliance on dream analysis as the crucial means of accessing the unconscious, but dreams do provide vivid moments and remain indicative of other clinical processes in the therapeutic work.

Dreams and creativity

It has been generally acknowledged in psychoanalysis that dreams and creativity originate from the same mental source and use the same unconscious processes. Khan put it succinctly when he said: "dreaming is prototypic of all psychic creativity" (Khan, 1962). Freud (1908e [1907]; 1923b) suggested that it is in the painful transition from the pleasure principle to the reality principle that instinctual gratification has to be renounced and fantasy and imagination are turned to providing substitutes. The neurotic finds these in day-dreaming, but the creative artist is able to turn fantasy and imagination—via the process of symbolization, amongst others—back into the world of reality in the form of cultural artefacts—novels, poetry, paintings. The neurotic and the artist are both trying to find compromise formations that represent the satisfactions of unconscious forces together with those of repression. The artist can sublimate the erotic impulses by transforming their aim and object into the creative process. For Freud, the erotic impulses are mainly the suppressed pre-genital, perverse, sexual excitations, which are transformed by sublimation so that they can be used for different cultural pursuits (Rayner, 1991).

In his later structural theory, and in conjunction with the development of his ideas on narcissism, particularly secondary narcissism, Freud continued to develop his thinking on this process. He suggested that the libidinal investment that people make in the object world is then withdrawn back into the ego. In this process of withdrawal, the original investment becomes desexualized, and so it is the narcissistic libido that is the source of the sublimated activity in creativity (Freud, 1914c).

In the psychoanalytic work influenced by the Independent group of psychoanalysts, there is a particular interest in dreaming, creativity, aesthetics, and the way these processes are part of, and emulate, the psychoanalytic process itself (Rayner, 1991). The work of Ella Freeman Sharpe, in the late 1930s, is one of these. Her seminal text, *Dream Analysis* (1937), was first prepared as a series of lectures for trainee analysts on the analysis of dreams. The book became "probably the best exposition of classical theory on dreams after Freud himself" (Rayner, 1991).

In this elegantly written text, Sharpe introduces important links between dreaming and creativity. Drawing on her understanding of literature and of literary criticism, she shows how the laws of poetic diction, formulated and codified from an intellectual survey of great poetry by critics, and the laws of dream formation, condensation, displacement, representability, and secondary revision come from the "same unconscious sources and have the same mechanisms in common" (Sharpe, 1937). She explains that the laws of poetic diction are inherent and intrinsic in the best verse and "so may be regarded as being the product of the closest co-operation between preconscious and unconscious activity". She shows how the task of the poet is to communicate by the sound and rhythms inherent in language and by the power of evoking imagery.

> To this end poetic diction prefers picturesque imagery to the enumeration of facts, it avoids the generic term and selects the particular. It is averse to lengthiness and dispenses with conjunction and relative pronoun where possible. It substitutes epithets for phrases. By means such as these a poem appeals to ear and eye and becomes an animated canvas. [Sharpe, 1937, p. 19]

The essays are brilliant illustrations of the way in which the visual perceptual world of the dream is translated into language for its telling. The language of the dream, the language in the dream, and the language used to tell the dream are based on the aesthetic laws of poetic diction. There is, for example, the simile—where two dissimilar things are equated by means of a common attribute: "Blue were her eyes as the fairy flax", is Sharpe's illustrative quotation. Metaphor is where the linking words "like" or "as" are left out, as, for example, in: "The ship ploughs the sea." There are also implied and personal metaphors, an example being an image of a hawk tearing at flesh in a dream implying destructive criticism; the idea of a babbling brook transfers human activities to the non-human. Metonymy is a form of condensation where a specific object stands for a general function: "the bar" or to "take silk" indicates the legal profession. Sharpe cites a patient's dream, *"I take a piece of silk from a cupboard and destroy it"*, to demonstrate his hatred of his legal profession; metonymy, she points out, is very common in dreams. Onomatopoeia and punning use the sounds of words for effect; synecdoche is where a part of a phrase, such as "all hands", does duty for a ship's company of men. The book is rich with illustrative material. As Khan (1978) says, Ella Sharpe was the first person to recognize that dream-work and the grammatical structure of language are of one and the same order, and her awareness of this predates the work of Jacques Lacan by decades.

Ella Freeman Sharpe and other British psychoanalysts (including her analysand Rycroft, who viewed psychoanalysis as primarily a linguistic discipline—Rayner, 1991) share features of a certain intellectual tradition that has its roots in the humanities, and many of the most original thinkers have an early background in the humanities. This has led to an abiding interest in the arts, creativity, and aesthetics. Within this framework of thought, the essential creativity in dreams is found to be closely linked to the creativity required to produce aesthetic objects of literature— novels and poetry—and of other art forms.

Ms Y

A patient of mine, a young woman artist, recently brought a dream that illustrates this point. In part of the dream *she was in her mother's house, watching her make a very intricate dress. She longed for her mother to make one for her, but she felt that she could not ask, and she knew that she would have to make her own, which would have to be plain, straight up and down, because that was all she could manage.* I said I thought she was longing for me to help her make sense to her of herself as she did not feel that she could do this for herself. She felt she could only make the simplest sense of herself, and that was nowhere near enough for her. She felt enormously guilty at the thought of wanting this from me, which helped us both to understand how much her mother had been unable to contain her and think about her as she was growing up. But then Ms Y went on to tell me how she had once made an installation/sculpture from a mould she had made of parts of her body, which she then reassembled and stitched together as an artefact. She felt deeply attached to it, but she told me that she has never really known where to place this work, in the same way that she does not really know what to do with herself. It was a vivid example of her desperate need to make herself over, to stitch herself together and find somewhere to put herself, but because of her inherent creativity she was able to make an artefact of some interest.

This clinical vignette of dreaming and creativity contrasts with further clinical material that appears later in the chapter and illustrates ideas on fantasy and day-dreaming where the day-dream is felt to be defensive (Trosman, 1995) and providing no more than a substitute gratification (Blum, 1976).

Dreams and sleep

There have been—and must continue to be—revisions of Freud's understanding of sleep and his view that dreams were the guardians of sleep: psycho/physiological work on sleep and dreaming was unknown in his day. Freud was, I think, less concerned with dreaming and its context and process than he was with the dream itself in terms of its structure and interpretation. For our purposes, it is the process of dreaming that is my focus.

Psychoanalysis is often accused of ignoring data from adjacent disciplines and fields of research—for example, from psychology and physiology—and there is little evidence that the work of sleep research has been taken much into consideration in psychoanalytic work on dreams and dreaming (Rayner, 1991). But some sleep researchers have been interested in psychoanalysis: the work of Richard Jones is of particular interest in this respect, as he is a practising psychoanalyst.

In his book, *The New Psychology of Dreaming* (Jones, 1970), he differentiates the neurophysiological state necessary for dreaming and the psychological phenomena of the dream. In the dream state, which appears to occur in all mammals, the individual, although asleep, is in a state of arousal. This state of arousal is recognized physiologically, through irregular pulse/blood pressure/respiration, rapid eye movement, penile erection, and sporadic activity of certain fine muscle groups. This has become known as Rapid Eye Movement (REM) sleep, as this is one of its key physical characteristics. This dream state occurs cyclically throughout the night, about every 90 minutes, and lasts for increasing amounts of time, from 5 to 40 minutes. When subjects are experimentally deprived of REM sleep by being repeatedly woken up during these phases of sleep, they deteriorate into a confused mental state more quickly than do subjects deprived of non-REM sleep. Rycroft has suggested that Freud's view that we dream in order to sleep needs to be reversed, in that perhaps we sleep in order to dream (Rycroft, 1979).

Dreaming, therefore, appears to be a response to arousal during sleep, of which REM is the most common indicator. But dreams can be a response to external stimulus such as the noise of an alarm clock, which is incorporated into the dream (Bateman & Holmes, 1995). Mentation is also reported in the non-REM state of sleep, but when this happens, the "dream" material is said to be apparently more cognitive, more governed by secondary process thinking, and therefore less open to interpretation (Jones, 1970).

The suggestion from this research is that neurophysiological factors are primary in the governance of sleep cycles. The dream state is not entirely governed by psychological processes; dreaming is therefore a result of some mutual facilitation between neuro-physiological and psychological functioning. Jones argues against Freud's view that the dream, like the neurotic symptom, encapsulates the infantile unconscious impulse and acts as a safety valve for the mind, so that the impulse is not discharged into action and sleep is maintained. In Jones's view, dreams can be seen as psychological activity—the mind is dealing with its processes and not discharging them. He even suggests that therapeutic work is going on in the dream and that dreaming itself is a therapeutic process.

In more recent work from neurophysiology, a paradigm of dreaming as information processing has been developed (Hobson, 1988, reported in Bateman & Holmes, 1995). In this paradigm, during sleep, the brain is ordering and storing the disparate memories and experiences stimulated by the recently activated neural pathways brought about by the day's events. In this model, "The bizarreness and vividness of dreams results from the random nature of the activation process . . . the dreaming brain is not struggling to disguise coherent but unacceptable thoughts, but to make sense of an array of chaotic imagery" (Bateman & Holmes, 1995).

All of this challenges many of the assumptions that have grown up around Freud's original thoughts on the purpose of dreams. When we are asleep and dreaming, according to Jones's conclusions, we are less asleep than the original theory would have had us be. We are asleep but aroused. It is in the non-dreaming state, in non-REM sleep, where there is reduced tension. The nature and function of sleeping and waking cannot therefore be taken so much for granted.

Khan (1962) outlines his view that Freud managed to create for the patient, in the psychoanalytic setting of a quiet room, couch, and analyst, a correspondence to the intra-psychic state in the dreamer that is "conducive to the good dream" (Khan, 1962). In this he is acknowledging and following through from the earlier views of Lewin (1955) who had seen the evolution of the hypnotic relationship into the analytic relationship as one of changing the patient from a hypnotic subject to a confider and the "magical sleep maker became a confidant. . . . The inference is that the analyst is the waker" (Lewin, 1955). The wish to be put to sleep is "supplanted by the wish to associate freely in the analytic situation" (Lewin, 1955). What is being suggested here is that there is an analogous relationship between the experience of the analytic session and the experience of dreaming.

Clifford M. Scott retained an interest in sleeping and waking in psychoanalysis throughout his long working life. He wanted to encourage psychoanalysts to write more about what it is like to be awake and what it is like to be asleep (Scott, 1988). He also wanted to understand more about the links between the sequences of sleeping and waking. He saw sleeping and waking as instincts, as did Freud (1940a [1938]), and he observed how these instincts could be in conflict, as in the symptoms of sleep-walking or sleep-talking. He said that the instincts can also be fused: "We can give a name to a sleeper who is dreaming with much greater ease than we can give a name to a wakeful person who is still much asleep and daydreams" (Scott, 1988), and that in learning to go to sleep and to wake up as quickly as we can, "we may forget the transitory states which, of course, we often do savour with pleasure but rarely talk about after infancy even in analysis. Babies babble themselves to sleep and learn to babble alone on waking" (Scott, 1988). It seems to me that later versions of this are the bedtime story for the older child and, later still, in adulthood the half-hour bedtime read of a not too demanding text before dropping off to sleep.

Transitory states; day-dreams; conscious fantasy

Scott's "pleasurable transitory states" (Scott, 1988) help us to move to a consideration of states of mind other than sleeping and waking and to consider the possibility of there being states of mind where the individual is neither asleep nor awake. Indeed, one could reflect further and wonder whether these concepts of sleep and wakefulness are describing true states of mental experience, or whether it would be more appropriate to think of them as theoretical constructs and that in fact no one is ever truly awake— or awake to being awake, as Scott puts it—and never truly asleep (Scott, 1988). However, at this point I will take it for granted that these states really exist in order to pursue the next stage of this discussion, which is to consider these transitory—or "in-between" sleeping and waking—states of mind. There is another concern that must be borne in mind at this point, which is to do with the differences, if any, between dreams and day-dreams and their inherent creativity or lack of it. In the following discussion I hope to be able to keep in mind the distinction between the different states of mind and their products.

In the language of psychoanalysis, in Britain, these differences are sometimes expressed in terms of spelling—namely, the use of "fantasy" to refer to more conscious mental processes, including day-dreams, and of "phantasy" to refer to the primary content of unconscious mental processes. This distinction evolved from the "Controversial Discussions", which took place in the British Psychoanalytic Society during the latter years of the Second World War (King & Steiner, 1991). I keep to this differentiation in this chapter.

Freud did not distinguish between fantasy and phantasy in the same way. As I mentioned earlier in the chapter, for Freud day-dreams share characteristics with dreams—they are wish-fulfilments based on infantile experiences, and for their expression they utilize the familiar dream structuring processes of displacement, condensation, representability, and secondary revision. This latter, secondary revision, has a greater role in consciously shaping these mental processes. This means that day-dreams and conscious fantasies have a greater consistency as stories than do dreams. This is particularly relevant to any understanding of the transitory states of being neither awake nor asleep mentioned earlier because, as Freud indicated, secondary revision is a working-over of the dream by "partly aroused waking thoughts" (Freud, 1900a).

In psychoanalysis there is no general agreement about the topographical position, in the mind, of a process like fantasy. Indeed, the very idea, in contemporary psychoanalysis, of maintaining the concept of the topographical model is a debatable issue. However, it has been argued (Sandler & Sandler, 1995) that it is possible to utilize aspects of the topographical model and the structural model of Freud's later work. For my purposes, it is useful to retain this spatial way of conceptualizing the mind, as I will be referring to other writers who have very usefully used concepts of internal space (Khan, 1972; Winnicott, 1951) to explain and describe the processes I am concerned with here.

Whilst Freud used the term fantasy/phantasy in different ways, he never fully discussed his thinking on this concept (Laplanche & Pontalis, 1973). When he wrote about unconscious phantasy, he seemed sometimes to be referring to a subliminal preconscious state of reverie of which the individual may or may not be consciously aware. Sometimes, as in Anna O's case, for example, the patient is quite conscious of their fantasies; at other times they are clearly the products of the unconscious. A common experience in psychotherapy is for a patient to say, after a silence, that their mind is a blank and they have no thoughts or imaginings. Closer investigation can often reveal a fleeting image or idea that will eventually enable a gradual uncovering of an otherwise quite unconscious phantasy.

It is in Freud's later work that he turns his attention to the nature and source of unconscious phantasy (Person, Figueira, & Fonagy, 1995). The most worked-out definition of phantasy appears in the metapsychology papers of 1915, where he suggests that, on the one hand, they would appear to "have made use of every acquisition of the system Cs. and would hardly be distinguished . . . from the formations of that system. On the other hand they are unconscious and are incapable of becoming conscious. Thus *qualitatively* they belong to the system PCs., but *factually* to the UCs. Their origin is what decides their fate" (Freud, 1915e, pp. 190–191). It would seem that he is more concerned to show the analogous relationship between the conscious and unconscious formations, the close relationship they share, and the transitions that take place between them than to justify or articulate the differences between them. In a much earlier paper, "Creative Writers and Day-Dreaming" (Freud, 1908e [1907]), he said that that daydreams and dreams are wish-fulfilments in "just the same way". He also said that day-dreams were the extension into adulthood of children's play: "We can never give anything up; we only exchange one thing for another" (Freud, 1908e [1907]).

In the *Three Essays* (1905d), Freud says that the conscious fantasies of perverts, the delusional fears of paranoiacs, and the unconscious phantasies that hysterics reveal behind their symptoms are identical in organization and content. Laplanche and Pontalis (1973) suggest the term *"une fantasmatique"* [a phantasmatic] for the structuring action of unconscious phantasy and its derivatives, on all aspects of the life of the individual—dreams, symptoms, acting out, repetitive behaviour, and so forth. They argue that it is important to recognize how the structuring actions of unconscious phantasy seek to express themselves and find their way into consciousness and action, constantly drawing into themselves new material.

Fantasies are scenarios, scenes, or scripts that are organized and capable of dramatization, often in a visual form, and usually directly expressible in language. Secondary revision means that impulses, wishes, and other mental products can be turned into a plausible story, a sequence of events in which the subject is present or is a witness of. Through the stories, desire is articulated, but fantasy is also a process by which defences are expressed, so that each fantasy is the story of desire and the story of prohibition.

In 1908 Freud concluded that "a happy person never phantasies, only an unsatisfied one. The motive forces of phantasies are unsatisfied wishes, and every single phantasy is the fulfilment of a wish, a correction of unsatisfying reality" (1908e [1907], p. 146). I would like to illustrate with some clinical material something of this and something of the relationship and connectedness between the conscious day-dream/fantasy and unconscious phantasy.

Mrs Z

Mrs Z, a young woman academic with a borderline personality disorder, was involved in a difficult, often angry and acrimonious relationship from which neither she nor her partner seemed able or willing to separate. The couple, as reported in the therapy, seemed intensely co-dependent. Their sexual life was nonexistent yet they longed for a child; they were deeply unhappy. The patient repeated the clinging dependency in the transference, often becoming ill during the breaks and weekends.

As the middle child of three and the only girl, Mrs Z had been subjected to serious violence from her disturbed father; the mother had apparently not intervened and had in fact joined with the father in blaming the child for her bad behaviour, which required punishment. Her siblings were no comfort to her, seeing her as frighteningly special and singled out. The father had been intensely focused on her, and there had inevitably been sexual excitement in their frequent violent encounters. Despite these experiences, she remained fond of her father, indicating a profound split, not only in her feelings for him but also in the way she had structured him in her inner world.

Mrs Z had a particularly concrete way of thinking in that she found it very difficult to use transference interpretations, although she had quite a clear intellectual understanding of what I was trying to help her to see when I made such interpretations. She really did feel that hostile imaginings and angry feelings towards me would damage me irreparably, and, given her intense dependence on me, this terrified her. She also experienced difficulty in using interpretations of her more positive feelings for me, as this reminded her of her need of me, which in turn frightened her very much. There was no transitional space between us in the therapy, no ability to maintain the "necessary state of 'virtuality'" (Bateman & Holmes, 1995) in relation to me. She had little capacity for symbolic thinking (Segal, 1957), as, for her, reality was so "saturated with phantasy that the two cannot be differentiated" (Bateman & Holmes, 1995). Needless to say, she rarely brought any dreams, so that when she began to report her day-dreams to me it seemed we might be making some progress.

Some time into her therapy Mrs Z began to tell me how she comforted herself in her unhappy and unfulfilled relationship by indulging in day-dreams of sexual relationships with her male colleagues, spending much of her time in this activity. On one occasion she was in the company of a colleague who was the current focus of these day-dreams and a woman colleague who announced that she was pregnant. She told me that this woman had been suddenly widowed a year or so earlier, when her husband had died in an accident. Her pregnancy was with her second husband. My patient was menstruating at the time and was extremely upset by this news. She told me that she was embarrassed and ashamed of the fantasies she could not stop having about her colleague, and she felt afraid that he would know that she had such desires towards him. She did not refer again to the dead husband, but as she was telling the story to me, I was almost distracted by an intense counter-transference experience of being in a hospital ward hearing dreadful news about a sudden and unexpected death. This was her own, projected unconscious phantasy of her deadly wishes towards her partner and towards me in the transference. I was able to show her how she had told me of her wish to have her partner/father/therapist dead so that she could have a baby with the man who was her colleague and the focus for her sexual desires, the man who was also the desired and loving partner/father/therapist. She was able for the first time to see the difference between a day-dream and a deeply unconscious wish. However, the shock of knowing about such a deadly wish led to some considerable disturbances in her behaviour and experiences over the ensuing weeks when we were both struggling with her almost psychotic fears.

Mrs Z's day-dreams of sex with other men were barely dis-guised wishes for her father, and the baby she longed for was the forbidden oedipal baby. She had always turned a deaf ear to such interpretations, which I had often made. Her fear and

her murderous rage towards her father were intensely defended against because of the psychotic qualities those feelings
contained; whenever there was any risk of her getting close to
such a state of mind, she felt she was going mad and was
terrified of being lost forever in the madness. All of this became vividly available for interpretation in the material I am
here reporting. She had a deeply hidden wish to kill off the
terrifying violent father so that she could be free of him—a
wish so frequently acted out in the bitter fighting with her
partner. Sexual intercourse with such a father would mean
mutual murder. She defended herself from this by her sexual
day-dreams with unavailable and forbidden men. Whenever
the day-dreams threatened to get close to reality, when, as
happened a few times, some of her men friends about whom
she fantasized approached her sexually, she became distraught
and ill with a variety of psychosomatic complaints, which were
always readily available.

Discussion

The in-between states of mind that I discussed earlier in this chapter have been conceptualized in somewhat different ways. Drawing on Winnicott's formulations, Khan (1972) discusses the way in
which patients can utilize, within inner psychic reality, the dream
space in which the healing processes of proper dreaming can be
actualized and brought usefully to the analysis. He suggests that
patients can use the dream space in the same way as the child uses
the transitional space of the paper to doodle on in the Squiggle
Game (Winnicott, 1971b).

In the same paper, Khan discusses what he refers to as the
abuse of the dream in psychic experience. He uses, as illustration,
one of Winnicott's patients—a middle-aged woman whose whole
life had been usurped and disturbed by fantasying or "something
of the nature of dreaming", which process was an "isolated phenomenon, absorbing energy but not contributing either to dreaming or to living" (Khan, 1972; Winnicott, 1971a). The patient was
engrossed by this and kept out of the world. Khan also discusses a

patient of his who "easily regressed to this type of dream-menta-
tion: a rapid conglomerate of bizarre images that scampered
through his head while he was reading, listening or watching. . . .
It only needed for him to be depersonalized a little from stress or
work to be taken over by it" (Khan, 1972). He explains that this
patient had established a dissociation in his personality, which
meant that he slipped away into this drowsy dream state without
having any control over the process. Khan shows how this was a
defence against very painful memories, and particularly unmanageable feelings of rage. The clinical vignette quoted above is also
an example of the same kind of difficulty. This kind of experience
is common in the more disturbed borderline patients who frequently speak of feeling absent, of not being there—"on the edge
of some remote universe, looking in", is how one patient put it to
me. These states of mind and experiences are frequently accompanied by feelings of anguish and often terror. For some patients, of
course, the dissociated state remains for a long time, and the conscious realization that this state is accompanied by incessant fantasies is only understood much later. Patients becoming aware of
this condition in themselves are beginning to emerge from their
psychic retreats (Steiner, 1993). When we are working with patients who are so ill, we understand that they can cushion themselves with such compulsive fantasying, as my patient did, and
we are aware what defensive structures they are and the deleteri-
ous effects they have on the mental resources the patients have at
their disposal. This is what I referred to at the beginning of this
chapter as a stultifying experience.

Conclusion

It is possible to establish an argument for the inherent creativity at
the heart of dreams and the mental processes involved in producing dreams. It can also be argued that these same mental processes, which the mind uses to structure dreams, do appear to be
the same as the poetic techniques creative artists use to structure
their work. We can say, then, that real creativity and dreaming
must be based on the same psychic processing.

We have also considered, via the context of dreams—namely sleep—that there are states of mind other than sleeping and waking. There are in-between states of mind, when we are neither asleep nor awake but in a state where dreams and the associative processes that can lead to creativity can flourish. Needless to say, this same in-between state can also be the deadened, going no-where place of a "psychic retreat" (Steiner, 1993).

In trying to make an aesthetic evaluation of the product of dreaming, the dream, and the product of fantasizing, the day-dream, the issues are not clear-cut. The very reflexivity in Freud's thinking on dreams and day-dreams makes it very difficult to theorize a qualitative difference between the two.

Clinicians are often equivocal about abstract thought, whether as theory or as clinical formulation, even though there must be a recognition of the importance of abstraction as an essential prerequisite for structuring thinking. The coming together of patient and therapist enables us to consider the two processes of dreaming and day-dreaming. Bringing the living patient back into our thoughts reveals a qualitative and serious difference between a dream and a day-dream. Free associations are not dreams. They are, in effect, conscious fantasies which, if they are lively enough and stimulate the clinician's mind, can lead to an interpretation. The revivifying power of an interpretation might be understood as the clinician being able to retell, for the patient, the real story of the dream and then both can know that real work is taking place.

REFERENCES AND BIBLIOGRAPHY

Aron, L. (1996). *A Meeting of Minds: Mutuality in Psychoanalysis.* Hillsdale, NJ/London: Analytic Press.

Bacelle, L. (1993). Working with psychotic patients. *Journal of Analytical Psychology, 38*: 13–22.

Badaracco, J. (1992). Psychic change and its clinical evaluation. *International Journal of Psycho-Analysis, 73*: 209–220.

Baker, R. (1993). The patient's discovery of the psychoanalyst as a new object. *International Journal of Psycho-Analysis, 74*: 1223–1233.

Balint, E. (1968). The Mirror and the Receiver. In: *Before I Was I* (pp. 56–62). London: Free Association Books, 1993.

Balint, M. (1968). *The Basic Fault: Therapeutic Aspects of Regression.* London: Tavistock Publications, 1984.

Balint, M. (1969). Trauma and object relationship. *International Journal of Psycho-Analysis, 50*: 429–435.

Barthes, R. (1977). *A Lover's Discourse.* New York: Farrar, Strauss & Giroux, 1978.

Bateman, A., & Holmes, J. (1995). *Introduction to Psychoanalysis.* London: Routledge.

Bergmann, M. (1994). The challenge of eroticised transference to psychoanalytic technique. *Psychoanalytic Inquiry, 14*: 499–518.

Bion, W. R. (1957). Differentiation of the psychotic from the non-psychotic personalities. *Second Thoughts. Selected Papers on Psycho-Analysis* (pp. 3–22). London: Heinemann, 1967. [Reprinted London: Karnac Books, 1984.]

Bion, W. R. (1959). Attacks on linking. *Second Thoughts. Selected Papers on Psycho-Analysis* (pp. 93–109). London: Heinemann, 1967. [Reprinted London: Karnac Books, 1984.]

Bion, W. R. (1977). *Two Papers: The Grid and Caesura.* London: Karnac Books, 1989.

Blum, H. (1976). The changing use of dreams in psychoanalytic practice: dreams and free association. *International Journal of Psycho-Analysis, 57*: 315–324.

Blum, H. (1994). The erotic transference: contemporary perspectives. *Psychoanalytic Inquiry, 14*: 622–635.

Bollas, C. (1987). *The Shadow of the Object: Psychoanalysis of the Unthought Known.* London: Free Association Books.

Bollas, C. (1989). *Forces of Destiny.* London: Free Association Books.

Bollas, C. (1993). *Being a Character.* London: Free Association Books.

Bollas, C. (1995). *Cracking Up.* London: Free Association Books.

Bollas, C. (1996). Figures and their functions: on the Oedipal structure of a psychoanalysis. *Psychoanalytic Quarterly, 65*: 1–20.

Bolognini, S. (1994). Transference: eroticised, erotic, loving, affectionate. *International Journal of Psycho-Analysis, 75*: 73–86.

Brenman-Pick, I. (1985). Working through in the countertransference. In: E. B. Spillius (Ed.), *Melanie Klein Today: Part 2: Mainly Practice.* London: Routledge.

Brenner, C. (1969). Dreams in clinical psychoanalytic practise. *Journal of Nervous & Mental Disease, 149.* [In: S. Flanders (Ed.), *The Dream Discourse Today* (pp. 49–63). London: Routledge, 1993.]

Britton, R. (1995). Reality and unreality in phantasy and fiction. In: S. Person, S. Figueira, & P. Fonagy (Eds.), *On Freud's "Creative Writers and Day-Dreaming".* New Haven, CT/London: Yale University Press.

Broucek, F. (1991). *Shame and the Self.* New York/London: Guildford Press.

Brown, L., Ed. (1993). *The New Shorter Oxford English Dictionary.* Oxford: Clarendon Press.

Casement, P. (1985). *On Learning from the Patient.* London: Tavistock.

Casement, P. (1987). The experience of trauma in the transference. In: J. Klauber et al., *Illusion and Spontaneity in Psychoanalysis* (pp. 79–98). London: Free Association Books, 1987.

Coltart, N. (1996). *The Baby and the Bathwater.* London: Karnac Books.

Cooper, J., & Maxwell, N. (Eds.) (1995). *Narcissistic Wounds: Clinical Perspectives.* London: Whurr Publishers.

Fabricius, J. (1995). The mutual search for self in the analytic dyad. *International Journal of Psycho-Analysis, 76:* 577–589.

Fairbairn, W. (1952). *Psychoanalytic Studies of the Personality.* London: Tavistock.

Ferenczi, S. (1913). Taming of a wild horse. In: *Final Contributions to the Problems and Methods of Psycho-Analysis* (pp. 336–341), ed. M. Balint, trans. E. Mosbacher. London: Hogarth Press, 1955. [Reprinted London: Karnac Books, 1994.]

Ferenczi, S. (1928). The elasticity of psychoanalytic technique. In: *Final Contributions to the Problems and Methods of Psycho-Analysis* (pp. 87–101), ed. M. Balint, trans. E. Mosbacher. London: Hogarth Press, 1955. [Reprinted London: Karnac Books, 1994.]

Ferenczi, S. (1930). The principles of relaxation and neocatharsis. In: *Final Contributions to the Problems and Methods of Psycho-Analysis* (pp. 108–125), ed. M. Balint, trans. E. Mosbacher. London: Hogarth Press, 1955. [Reprinted London: Karnac Books, 1994.]

Ferenczi, S. (1931). Child-analysis in the analysis of adults. In: *Final Contributions to the Problems and Methods of Psycho-Analysis* (pp. 126–142), ed. M. Balint, trans. E. Mosbacher. London: Hogarth Press, 1955.

Ferenczi, S. (1932). *The Clinical Diary of Sándor Ferenczi,* ed. J. Dupont, trans. M. Balint & N. Z. Jackson. Cambridge, MA: Harvard University Press, 1985.

Ferenczi, S. (1933). Confusion of tongues between adults and the child. In: *Final Contributions to the Problems and Methods of Psycho-Analysis* (pp. 156–167), ed. M. Balint, trans. E. Mosbacher. London: Hogarth Press, 1955. [Reprinted London: Karnac Books, 1994.]

Flanders, S. (Ed.) (1993). *The Dream Discourse Today.* London: Routledge.

Fonagy, P., Moran, G., Edgcumbe, R., Kennedy, H., & Target, M. (1993). The roles of mental representations and mental processes in therapeutic action. *Psychoanalytic Study of the Child, 48:* 9–48.

Fonagy, P., Moran, G., & Target, M. (1993). Aggression and the psychological self. *International Journal of Psycho-Analysis 74:* 471–485.

Frank, A. (1991). Psychic change and the analyst as biographer: transference and reconstruction. *International Journal of Psycho-Analysis, 72:* 22–26.

Freud, S. (1893a). On the psychical mechanism of hysterical phenomena. In: J. Strachey (Ed.), *Standard Edition of the Complete Psycho-*

logical Works of Sigmund Freud, Vol. 3 (pp. 25–40). London: Hogarth Press, 1950–1974.

Freud, S. (1895d) (with Breuer, J.). *Studies on Hysteria. S.E., Vol. 2.*

Freud, S. (1900a). *The Interpretation of Dreams. S.E., Vols. 4 & 5.*

Freud, S. (1905d). *Three Essays on the Theory of Sexuality.* In: *S.E., Vol. 7* (pp. 135–243).

Freud, S. (1908e [1907]). Creative writers and day-dreaming. In: *S.E., Vol. 9* (pp. 143–153).

Freud, S. (1910a [1909]). *Five Lectures on Psycho-Analysis.* In: *S.E., Vol. 11,* (pp. 9–55).

Freud, S. (1910d). The future prospects of psycho-analytic psychotherapy. In: *S.E., Vol. 11* (pp. 141–151).

Freud, S. (1912b). The dynamics of transference. In: *S.E., Vol. 12* (pp. 97–108).

Freud, S. (1912e). Recommendations to physicians practising psychoanalysis. *S.E., Vol. 12* (pp. 111–120).

Freud, S. (1913c). On beginning the treatment. In: *S.E., Vol. 12* (pp. 123–141).

Freud, S. (1914c). On narcissism: an introduction. In: *S.E., Vol. 14* (pp. 67–102).

Freud, S. (1914g). Remembering, repeating and working through. In: *S.E., Vol. 12* (pp. 147–156).

Freud, S. (1915a). Observations on transference love. In: *S.E., Vol. 12* (pp. 159–171).

Freud, S. (1915e). The unconscious. In: *S.E., Vol. 14* (pp. 166–215).

Freud, S. (1918 [1914]). From the history of an infantile neurosis. In: *S.E., Vol. 17* (pp. 1–122).

Freud, S. (1920g). *Beyond the Pleasure Principle.* In: *S.E., Vol. 18* (pp. 7–64).

Freud, S. (1921c). *Group Psychology and the Analysis of the Ego.* In: *S.E., Vol. 18* (pp. 65–143).

Freud, S. (1923b). *The Ego and the Id.* In: *S.E., Vol. 19* (pp. 12–66).

Freud, S. (1924b [1923]). Neurosis and psychosis. In: *S.E., Vol. 19* (pp. 149–153).

Freud, S. (1926d [1925]). *Inhibitions, Symptoms and Anxiety.* In: *S.E., Vol. 20* (pp. 87–174).

Freud, S. (1927e). Fetishism. In: *S.E., Vol. 21* (pp. 152–157).

Freud, S. (1932e [1931]). Preface to the Third Edition of *The Interpretation of Dreams.*

Freud, S. (1933a). *New Introductory Lectures on Psycho-Analysis. S.E., Vol. 22.*

Freud, S. (1933a). Lecture 34, Explanations, applications and orientations. In: *New Introductory Lectures on Psycho-Analysis. S.E., Vol. 22* (pp. 136–157).

Freud, S. (1940a [1938]). *An Outline of Psycho-Analysis.* In: *S.E., Vol. 23* (pp. 144–207).

Freud, S. (1940e [1938]). Splitting of the ego in the process of defence. In: *S.E., Vol. 23* (pp. 275–278).

Gabbard, G. (1995). Countertransference: the emerging common ground. *International Journal of Psycho-Analysis, 76*: 475–485.

Giovacchini, P. (1979). *Treatment Issues in Treatment of Primitive Mental States.* New York: Jason Aronson.

Greenson, R. (1974). *The Technique and Practice of Psycho-Analysis, Vol. 1.* London: Hogarth Press.

Grinberg, L. (1978). The razor's edge in depression and mourning. *International Journal of Psycho-Analysis, 59*: 245–254. [In: *The Goals of Psychoanalysis* (pp. 171–190). London: Karnac Books, 1990.]

Grinberg, M. (1997). Is the transference feared by the psychoanalyst? *International Journal of Psycho-Analysis, 78*: 1–14.

Grotstein, J. (1985). *Splitting and Projective Identification.* New York: Jason Aronson, 1986.

Guntrip, H. (1975). My experience of analysis with Fairbairn and Winnicott. *International Review of Psycho-Analysis, 2*: 145–156.

Hamilton, V. (1996). *The Analyst's Preconscious.* Hillsdale, NJ/London: Analytic Press.

Haynal, A. (1989). The concept of trauma and its present meaning. *International Journal of Psycho-Analysis, 16*: 315–321.

Heimann, P. (1949–50). On counter-transference. *International Journal of Psycho-Analysis, 31*: 81–84. [In: *About Children and Children-No-Longer* (pp. 73–79), ed. M. Tonnesmann. London: Routledge, 1989.]

Heimann, P. (1957–59). Some notes on sublimation. *About Children and Children-No-Longer* (pp. 122–137), ed. M. Tonnesmann. London: Routledge, 1989.

Hill, D. (1994). Special place of the erotic transference in psychoanalysis. *Psychoanalytic Inquiry, 14*: 483–498.

Hobson, J. (1988). *The Dreaming Brain.* London: Penguin.

Jacobs, T. (1993). The inner experiences of the analyst: their contribution to the analytic process. *International Journal of Psycho-Analysis, 74*: 7-14.

Jenkins, M. (1995). "Further thoughts on the concept of two selves." Public lecture at the Highgate Literary and Scientific Institute, London.

Jones, R. (1970). *The New Psychology of Dreaming.* New York: Grune & Stratton.

Joseph, B. (1985). Transference: the total situation. *International Journal of Psycho-Analysis, 66*: 447–454. [In: E. B. Spillius (Ed.), *Melanie Klein Today, Vol. 2: Mainly Practice* (pp. 61–72). London: Routledge.]

Khan, M. (1962). Dream psychology and the evolution of the psychoanalytic situation. *International Journal of Psycho-Analysis, 43*. [In: *The Privacy of the Self* (pp. 27–41). London: Karnac Books. *The Dream Discourse Today*, ed. S. Flanders. London: Routledge.]

Khan, M. (1964). Ego distortion, cumulative trauma, and the role of reconstruction in the analytic situation. *International Journal of Psycho-Analysis, 45*: 272–279. [In: *The Privacy of the Self* (pp. 59–68). London: Karnac Books.]

Khan, M. (1972). The use and abuse of dream in psychic experience. *International Journal of Psychoanalytic Psychotherapy, 13*. [In: *The Privacy of the Self* (pp. 306–315). London: Karnac Books. *The Dream Discourse Today*, ed. S. Flanders. London: Routledge.]

Khan, M. (1975). Introduction. In: D. W. Winnicott, *Through Paediatrics to Psycho-Analysis* (pp. xi–xlix). London: Hogarth Press and The Institute of Psycho-Analysis, 1982. [Reprinted London: Karnac Books, 1992.]

Khan, M. (1978). Introduction. In: E. Freeman Sharpe, *Dream Analysis* (second edition). London: Hogarth Press. [Reprinted London: Karnac Books, 1988.]

Khan, M. (1979). *Alienation in Perversions*. London: Hogarth Press. [Reprinted London: Karnac Books, 1993.]

King, P. (1978). Affective response of the analyst to the patient's communications. *International Journal of Psycho-Analysis, 59*: 329–334.

King, P., & Steiner, R. (Eds.) (1991). *The Freud–Klein Controversies. 1941–45*. London: Routledge.

Klauber, J. (1967). Reporting dreams in psychoanalysis. *Difficulties in the Analytic Encounter* (pp. 3–24). London: Free Association Books, 1986. [Reprinted London: Karnac Books, 1986.]

Klauber, J. (1986). *Difficulties in the Analytic Encounter*. London: Free Association Books. [Reprinted London: Karnac Books, 1986.]

Klein, M. (1948). *Contributions to Psycho-Analysis*. London: Hogarth Press.

Kohon, G. (Ed.) (1986a). *The British School of Psychoanalysis: The Independent Tradition*. London: Free Association Books.

Kohon, G. (1986b). Countertransference: an Independent view. In: *The British School of Psychoanalysis: The Independent Tradition*. London: Free Association Books.

Kohut, H. (1984). *How Does Analysis Cure?* Chicago, IL: University of Chicago Press.

Laplanche, J. (1989). The practical task. In: *New Foundations for Psychoanalysis* (pp. 152–164). Oxford/Cambridge: Basil Blackwell.

Laplanche, J., & Pontalis, J. (1973). *The Language of Psycho-Analysis.* London: Hogarth Press, 1973. [Reprinted London: Karnac Books, 1988.]

Levine, H. (1994). The analyst's participation in the analytic process. *International Journal of Psycho-Analysis, 75:* 665–676.

Lewin, B. (1946). Sleep, the mouth and the dream screen. *Psychoanalytic Quarterly, 15:* 419.

Lewin, B. (1955). Dream psychology and the analytic situation. *Psychoanalytic Quarterly, 24.*

Lucas, R. (1993). The psychotic wavelength. *Psychoanalytic Psychotherapy, 7:* 15–24.

March, P. (1997). In two minds about cognitive–behaviour therapy: talking to patients about why they do not do their homework. *British Journal of Psychotherapy, 13:* 461–472.

McDougall, J. (1989). *Theatres of the Body.* Hillsdale, NJ/London: Free Association Books.

Miller, J. (1983). *States of Mind.* London: BBC.

Monchaux de, C. (1978). Dreaming and the organising function of the ego. *International Journal of Psycho-Analysis, 59:* 443–453.

Money-Kyrle, R. (1955). Normal counter-transference and some of its deviations. In: E. B. Spillius (Ed.), *Melanie Klein Today, Part 2: Mainly Practice.* London: Routledge.

Money-Kyrle, R. (1971). The aim of psycho-analysis. *International Journal of Psycho-Analysis, 52:* 103–106. [In: *The Collected Papers of Roger Money-Kyrle* (pp. 442–429). Perthshire: Clunie Press, 1978.]

Ogden, T. (1985). On potential space. *International Journal of Psycho-Analysis, 66:* 127–142. [In: *The Matrix of the Mind* (pp. 208–232). London: Karnac Books, 1992.]

Person, S. (1995). Introduction. In: S. Person, S. Figueira, & P. Fonagy (Eds.), *On Freud's "Creative Writers and Day-Dreaming".* New Haven, CT: Yale University Press.

Person, S., Figueira, S., Fonagy, P. (1995). *On Freud's "Creative Writers and Day-Dreaming".* New Haven, CT: Yale University Press.

Racker, H. (1968). *Transference and Countertransference.* London: Hogarth Press. [Reprinted London: Karnac Books, 1982.]

Rappaport, E. (1956). The management of an eroticised transference. *Psychoanalytic Quarterly, 25:* 515–529.

Rayner, E. (1991). *The Independent Mind in British Psychoanalysis.*

Northvale, NJ/London: Jason Aronson; London: Free Association Books.

Richards, J. (1993). Cohabitation and the negative therapeutic reaction. *Psychoanalytic Psychotherapy*, 7: 223–239.

Richards, J. (1994). The flight from health. *Journal of the British Association of Psychotherapists*, 26: 65–81.

Richards, J. (1995). Narcoleptic states in psychoanalytic psychotherapy. *British Journal of Psychotherapy*, 11: 546–556.

Rosenfeld, H. (1987). *Impasse and Interpretation*. London/New York: Routledge; London: Tavistock.

Roth, P. (1988). "The effective interpretation: its formulation and its reception." Paper presented at the English-Speaking Conference.

Rowan, J. (1990). *Subpersonalities*. London: Routledge.

Rycroft, C. (1979). *The Innocence of Dreams*. London: Hogarth Press.

Sandler, J. (1960). The background of safety. *International Journal of Psycho-Analysis*, 41: 352–356.

Sandler, J. (1976). Countertransference and role responsiveness. *International Review of Psycho-Analysis*, 3: 43–47.

Sandler, J. (1993). On communication from patient to analyst: not everything is projective identification. *International Journal of Psycho-Analysis*, 74: 1097–1107.

Sandler, A. M., & Sandler, J. (1995). Unconscious phantasy, identification, and projection in the creative writer. In: S. Person, S. Figueira, & P. Fonagy (Eds.), *On Freud's "Creative Writers and Day-Dreaming"*. New Haven, CT: Yale University Press.

Scott, C. (1988). Repairing broken links. *Free Associations*, 12.

Searles, H. F. (1951). Data concerning certain manifestations of incorporation. In: *Collected Papers on Schizophrenia and Related Subjects* (pp. 39–69), 1965.

Searles, H. F. (1952). Concerning a psychodynamic function of perplexity, confusion, suspicion, and related mental states. In: *Collected Papers on Schizophrenia and Related Subjects* (pp. 70–113), 1965.

Searles, H. F. (1959). Oedipal love in the countertransference. *International Journal of Psycho-Analysis*, 40: 180–190. [In: *Collected Papers on Schizophrenia and Related Subjects* (pp. 284–303), 1965.]

Searles, H. F. (1961). Phases of patient–therapist interaction in the psychotherapy of chronic schizophrenia. In: *Collected Papers on Schizophrenia and Related Subjects* (pp. 521–559), 1965.

Searles, H. F. (1965). *Collected Papers on Schizophrenia and Related Subjects*. London: Hogarth Press. [Reprinted London: Karnac Books, 1986.]

Segal, H. (1952). A psychoanalytic approach to aesthetics. In: *The Work of Hanna Segal*. New York: Jason Aronson, 1981.

Segal, H. (1957). Notes on symbol fomation. *International Journal of Psycho-Analysis*, 38: 391–397.

Segal, H. (1981). *The Work of Hanna Segal*. New York: Jason Aronson.

Sharpe, E. Freeman (1937). *Dream Analysis*. London: Hogarth Press. [Reprinted with Introduction by Masud Khan, 1978. Reprinted London: Karnac Books, 1988.]

Shorter Oxford English Dictionary. Oxford: Clarendon Press, 1973, Volume 2.

Shorter Oxford English Dictionary on Historical Principles (1991). Oxford: Clarendon Press.

Sinason, M. (1993). Who is the mad voice inside? In: *Psychoanalytic Psychotherapy*, 7: 207–221.

Sinason, M. (1997). "The monsterising of jealousy and envy—a case of mistaken identity." The first Martin Jenkins Annual Memorial Lecture, Arbours Association.

Steiner, J. (1993). *Psychic Retreats*. London: Routledge.

Stern, D. (1990). *Diary of a Baby*. New York: Basic Books.

Stewart, H. (1973). Dream and transference. *Psychic Experience and Problems of Technique*. London: Routledge, 1992.

Strachey, J. (1934). The nature of the therapeutic action of psychoanalysis. *International Journal of Psycho-Analysis*, 15: 127–159.

Symington, N. (1996). *The Making of a Psychotherapist*. London: Karnac Books.

Tonnesmann, M. (Ed.) (1989). *About Children and Children-No-Longer. Collected Papers 1942–80 of Paula Heimann*. London: Routledge.

Trosman, H. (1995). A modern view of Freud's "Creative Writers and Day-Dreaming". In: S. Person, S. Figueira, & P. Fonagy (Eds.), *On Freud's "Creative Writers and Day-Dreaming"*. New Haven, CT: Yale University Press.

Tustin, F. (1981). Psychological birth and psychological catastrophe. In: *Do I Dare Disturb the Universe?*, ed. J. Grotstein. London: Caesura Press. [Reprinted with corrections London: Karnac Books, 1983.]

Winnicott, D. W. (c. 1939). Aggression. In: *The Child and the Outside World* (pp. 167–175). London: Tavistock Publications, 1957.

Winnicott, D. W. (1947). Further thoughts on babies as persons. In: *The Child and the Outside World* (pp. 134–140). London: Tavistock Publications, 1957.

Winnicott, D. W. (1948). Paediatrics and psychiatry. In: *Collected Papers: Through Paediatrics to Psycho-Analysis*. London: Tavistock,

1958; New York: Basic Books, 1958. [Reprinted as *Through Paediatrics to Psycho-Analysis* (pp. 157–173), 1975.]

Winnicott, D. W. (1950). The deprived child and how he can be compensated for loss of family life. In: *The Family and Individual Development* (pp. 132–145). London: Tavistock, 1965. [Reprinted in: *Deprivation and Delinquency*, ed. C. Winnicott, R. Shepherd, & M. Davis. London: Tavistock, 1984; New York: Methuen, 1984.]

Winnicott, D. W. (1950–55). Aggression in relation to emotional development. In: *Collected Papers: Through Paediatrics to Psycho-Analysis*. London: Tavistock, 1958; New York: Basic Books, 1958. [Reprinted as *Through Paediatrics to Psycho-Analysis* (pp. 204–210), 1975.]

Winnicott, D. W. (1951). Transitional objects and transitional phenomena. In: *Collected Papers: Through Paediatrics to Psycho-Analysis*. London: Tavistock, 1958; New York: Basic Books, 1958. [Reprinted as *Through Paediatrics to Psycho-Analysis* (pp. 229–242), 1975.]

Winnicott, D. W. (1952a). Anxiety associated with insecurity. In: *Collected Papers: Through Paediatrics to Psycho-Analysis*. London: Tavistock, 1958; New York: Basic Books, 1958. [Reprinted as *Through Paediatrics to Psycho-Analysis* (pp. 97–100), 1975.]

Winnicott, D. W. (1952b). Psychoses and child care. In: *Collected Papers: Through Paediatrics to Psycho-Analysis*. London: Tavistock, 1958; New York: Basic Books, 1958. [Reprinted as *Through Paediatrics to Psycho-Analysis* (pp. 219–228), 1975.]

Winnicott, D. W. (1955a). Adopted children in adolescence. In: *Thinking About Children* (pp. 136–148), ed. R. Shepherd, J. Johns, & H. Taylor Robinson. London: Karnac Books, 1996; Reading, MA: Addison-Wesley, 1996.

Winnicott, D. W. (1955b). Clinical varieties of transference. In: *Collected Papers: Through Paediatrics to Psycho-Analysis*. London: Tavistock, 1958; New York: Basic Books, 1958. [Reprinted as *Through Paediatrics to Psycho-Analysis* (pp. 295–299), 1975.]

Winnicott, D. W. (1957). The mother's contribution to society. In: *The Child and the Family*. London: Tavistock, 1957. [Reprinted in: *Home Is Where We Start From*, ed. C. Winnicott, R. Shepherd, & M. Davis. London: Penguin, 1986. Also reprinted in: *The Child and the Family: First Relationships* (pp. 141–144), ed. J. Hardenberg. London: Tavistock Publications.]

Winnicott, D. W. (1958). The capacity to be alone. In: *The Maturational Processes and the Facilitating Environment: Studies in the Theory of Emotional Development* (pp. 29–36), 1965.

Winnicott, D. W. (1960a). Aggression, guilt and reparation. In: *Deprivation and Delinquency*, ed. C. Winnicott, R. Shepherd, & M. Davis.

London; Tavistock, 1984. New York: Methuen, 1984. [Reprinted in: *Home Is Where We Start From* (pp. 80–89), ed. C. Winnicott, R. Shepherd, & M. Davis. London: Penguin, 1986; New York: W. W. Norton, 1986.]

Winnicott, D. W. (1960b). Ego distortion in terms of true and false self. In: *The Maturational Processes and The Facilitating Environment: Studies in the Theory of Emotional Development* (pp. 140–152), 1965.

Winnicott, D. W. (1960c). The relationship of a mother to her baby at the beginning [rewritten 1964]. In: *The Family and Individual Development* (pp. 15–20). London: Tavistock, 1965.

Winnicott, D. W. (1960d). The theory of the parent–infant relationship. *International Journal of Psycho-Analysis, 41*: 585–595. [In: *The Maturational Processes and the Facilitating Environment: Studies in the Theory of Emotional Development* (pp. 37–55), 1965.]

Winnicott, D. W. (1962). Ego integration in child development. In: *The Maturational Processes and the Facilitating Environment: Studies in the Theory of Emotional Development* (pp. 56–63), 1965.

Winnicott, D. W. (1964). Roots of aggression. In: *The Child, the Family and the Outside World* (pp. 232–239). London: Penguin, 1964; Reading, MA: Addison-Wesley, 1987.

Winnicott, D. W. (1965). *The Maturational Processes and the Facilitating Environment: Studies in the Theory of Emotional Development.* London: Hogarth Press & The Institute of Psycho-Analysis. [Reprinted London: Karnac Books, 1990.]

Winnicott, D. W. (1971a). *Playing and Reality.* London: Tavistock, 1971; New York: Methuen, 1982.

Winnicott, D. W. (1971b). *Therapeutic Consultations in Child Psychiatry.* London: Hogarth Press & The Institute of Psycho-Analysis; New York: Basic Books.

Winnicott, D. W. (1975). *Through Paediatrics to Psycho-Analysis* (pp. 157–173). London: Hogarth Press & The Institute of Psycho-Analysis. [Reprinted London: Karnac Books, 1992.]

Winnicott, D. W. (1989). *Psycho-Analytic Explorations,* ed. C. Winnicott, R. Shepherd, & M. Davis. London: Karnac Books; Cambridge, MA: Harvard University Press.

Winnicott, D. W. (1996). *Thinking about Children,* ed. R. Shepherd, J. Johns, & H. Taylor Robinson. London: Karnac Books; Reading, MA: Addison-Wesley.

Zetzel, E. (1970). *The Capacity for Emotional Growth.* New York: International Universities Press. [Reprinted London: Karnac Books, 1989.]

INDEX

acting out, in countertransference, 5, 104, 116, 117, 122, 123
adoption, 13–26
aesthetics, 154, 156
aggression, 5
    Winnicott on, 92–94
analysis, mutual, 126
analytic neutrality of therapist, 2, 3, 10, 21, 24–25, 134–135
Anna O [Breuer], 33, 161
anxieties, unthinkable [Winnicott], 55, 56
Aron, L., 120, 121, 125
arts, 156
attachment, oral aspect of, 74

baby (infant):
    no such thing as [Winnicott], 2
    undifferentiation of, 53, 77
Bacelle, L., 38
Badaracco, J., 67
Baker, R., 116, 117, 118, 121, 122, 123, 130

Balint, E., 69
Balint, M., 98
    "basic fault", 2, 57
    on regressed patient, 18
    on trauma, 5, 111–131
Barthes, R., 133
"basic fault" [Balint], 2, 57
Bateman, A., 158, 163, 164
Bergmann, M., 134
Berkowitz, R., xi, 5, 111–131
Bion, W. R., 2, 33–36, 98, 131
    on psychotic vs. non-psychotic personality, 34, 41
bipolar illness, 41
Blum, H., 140, 157
Bollas, C., 66, 115, 116, 121, 123, 128, 129, 130
Bolognini, S., 140
borderline states, 33, 39, 56, 73, 166
Brenman-Pick, I., 116, 118
Brenner, C., 153
Breuer, J., 32
    Anna O, 33, 161